Galatians

Amazing Grace

JOHN A. STEWART

Lamplighters International is a Christian ministry that helps individuals engage with God and His Word and equips believers to be disciple-makers.

For additional information about Lamplighters ministry resources, contact:

Lamplighters International
771 NE Harding Street, Suite 250
Minneapolis, MN USA 55413
or visit our website at
www.LamplightersUSA.org.

Product Code Ga-NK-SS

ISBN 978-1-931372-63-3

CONTENTS

How to Use This Study

WHAT IS LAMPLIGHTERS?

Lamplighters International is an evangelical Christian ministry that publishes Christ-centered, Bible-based curriculum and trains believers to be intentional disciple makers. This Bible study, comprising eleven individual lessons, is a self-contained unit and an integral part of the entire discipleship ministry. When you have completed the study, you will have a much greater understanding of a portion of God's Word, with many new truths that you can apply to your life.

HOW TO STUDY A LAMPLIGHTERS LESSON

A Lamplighters study begins with prayer, your Bible, the weekly lesson, and a sincere desire to learn more about God's Word. The questions are presented in a progressive sequence as you work through the study material. You should not use Bible commentaries or other reference books (except a dictionary) until you have completed your weekly lesson and met with your weekly group. Approaching the Bible study in this way allows you to personally encounter many valuable spiritual truths from the Word of God.

To gain the most out of the Bible study, find a quiet place to complete your weekly lesson. Each lesson will take approximately 45–60 minutes to complete. You will likely spend more time on the first few lessons until you are familiar with the format, and our prayer is that each week will bring the discovery of important life principles.

The writing space within the weekly studies provides the opportunity for you to answer questions and respond to what you have learned. Putting answers in your own words, and including Scripture references where appropriate, will help you personalize and commit to memory the truths you have learned. The answers to the questions will be found in the Scripture references at the end of each question or in the passages listed at the beginning of each lesson.

If you are part of a small group, it's a good idea to record the specific dates that you'll be meeting to do the individual lessons. Record the specific dates each time the group will be meeting next to the lesson titles on the Contents page. Additional lines have been provided for you to record when you go through this same study at a later date.

The side margins in the lessons can be used for the spiritual insights you glean from other group or class members. Recording these spiritual truths will likely be a spiritual help to you and others when you go through this study again in the future.

Audio Introduction

A brief audio introduction is available to help you learn about the historical background of the book, gain an understanding of its theme and structure, and be introduced to some of the major truths. Audio introductions are available for all Lamplighters studies and are a great resource for the group leader; they can also be used to introduce the study to your group. To access the audio introductions, go to www.LamplightersUSA.org.

"Do You Think?" Questions

Each weekly study has a few "do you think?" questions designed to help you to make personal applications from the biblical truths you are learning. In the first lesson the "do you think?" questions are placed in italic print for easy identification. If you are part of a study group, your insightful answers to these questions could be a great source of spiritual encouragement to others.

Personal Questions

Occasionally you'll be asked to respond to personal questions. If you are part of a study group you may choose not to share your answers to these questions with the others. However, be sure to answer them for your own benefit because they will help you compare your present level of spiritual maturity to the biblical principles presented in the lesson.

A Final Word

Throughout this study the masculine pronouns are frequently used in the generic sense to avoid awkward sentence construction. When the pronouns he, him, and his are used in reference to the Trinity (God the Father, Jesus Christ, and the Holy Spirit), they always refer to the masculine gender.

This Lamplighters study was written after many hours of careful preparation. It is our prayer that it will help you "… grow in the grace and knowledge of our Lord and Savior Jesus Christ. To Him be the glory both now and forever. Amen" (2 Peter 3:18).

What Is an Intentional Discipleship Bible Study?

The *Next Step* in Bible Study

The Lamplighters Bible study series is ideal for individual, small group, and classroom use. This Bible study is also designed for Intentional Discipleship training. An Intentional Discipleship (ID) Bible study has four key components. Individually they are not unique, but together they form the powerful core of the ID Bible study process.

1. Objective: Lamplighters is a discipleship training ministry that has a dual objective: (1) to help individuals engage with God and His Word and (2) to equip believers to be disciple-makers. The small group format provides extensive opportunity for ministry training, and it's not limited by facilities, finances, or a lack of leadership staffing.

2. Content: The Bible is the focus rather than Christian books. Answers to the study questions are included within the study guides, so the theology is in the study material, not in the leader's mind. This accomplishes two key objectives: (1) It gives the group leader confidence to lead another individual or small group without fear, and (2) it protects the small group from theological error.

3. Process: The ID Bible study process begins with an Open House, which is followed by a 6–14-week study, which is followed by a presentation of the Final Exam (see graphic on page 8). This process provides a natural environment for continuous spiritual growth and leadership development.

4. Leadership Development: As group participants grow in Christ, they naturally invite others to the groups. The leader-trainer (1) identifies and recruits new potential leaders from within the group, (2) helps them register for online discipleship training, and (3) provides in-class leadership mentoring until they are both competent and confident to lead a group according to the ID Bible study process. This leadership development process is scalable, progressive, and comprehensive.

Overview of the Leadership Training and Development Process

There are three stages of leadership training in the Intentional Discipleship process: (1) leading studies, (2) training leaders, and (3) multiplying groups (see appendix for greater detail).

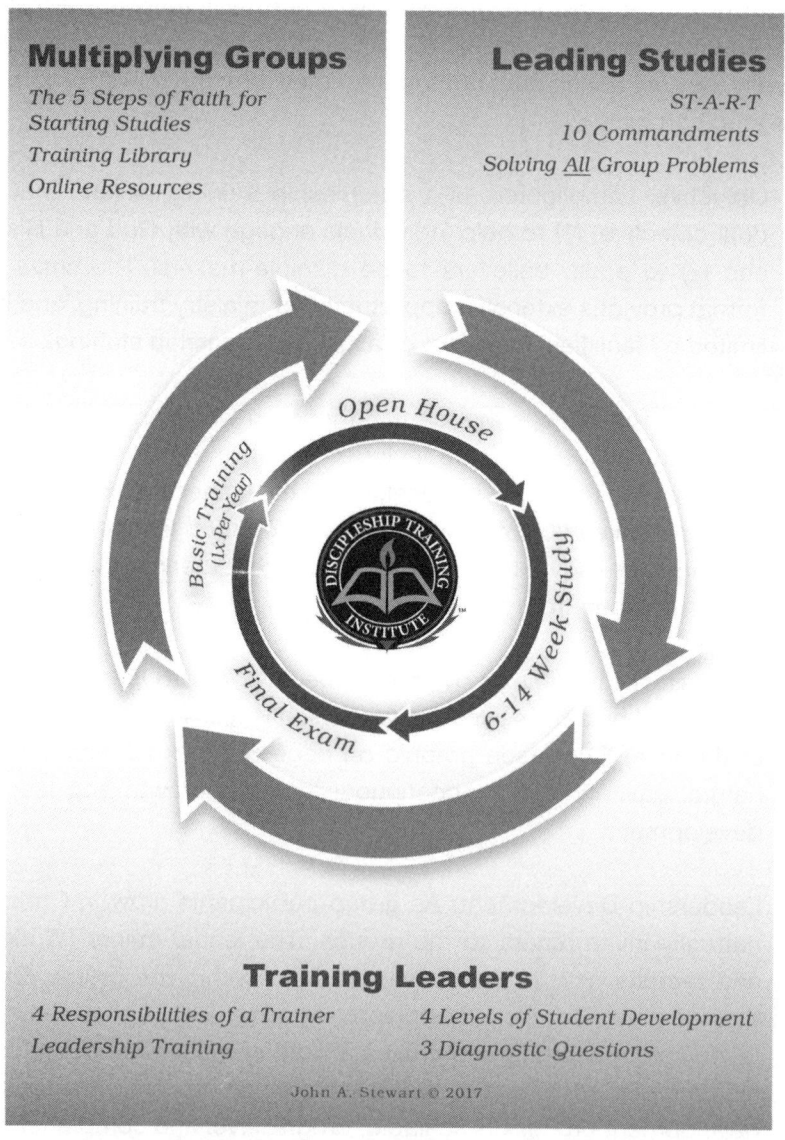

Multiplying Groups

The 5 Steps of Faith for Starting Studies

Training Library

Online Resources

Leading Studies

ST-A-R-T

10 Commandments

Solving All Group Problems

Open House

Basic Training (1x Per Year)

6-14 Week Study

Final Exam

DISCIPLESHIP TRAINING INSTITUTE

Training Leaders

4 Responsibilities of a Trainer

Leadership Training

4 Levels of Student Development

3 Diagnostic Questions

John A. Stewart © 2017

How Can I Be Trained?

Included within this Bible study is the student workbook for Level 1 (Basic Training). Level 1 training is both free and optional. Level 1 training teaches you a simple 4-step process (ST-A-R-T) to help you prepare a life-changing Bible study and 10 proven small group leadership principles that will help your group thrive. To register for a Level 1 online training event, either as an individual or as a small group, go to www.LamplightersUSA.org/training or www.discipleUSA.org. If you have additional questions, you can also call 800-507-9516.

INTRODUCTION

The Protestant Reformation (1517–1648) brought the rediscovery of salvation by grace and exposed the tyranny of religious oppression. The book of Galatians was the cornerstone of the Reformation because it clearly taught the relationship between law and grace and the freedom available to all who come to saving faith in Christ. Reformer Martin Luther loved the book of Galatians and called it his Catherine Von Bora (his wife's name) for, he said, "I am wedded to it."

The fires of the Reformation were still burning when the Pilgrims brought religious freedom to America. John Wesley, whose Methodist movement had a significant influence on American colonial life, was converted to Christ through the influence of Martin Luther. Some church historians believe the book of Galatians has influenced the thinking of the Western World more than any other written document.

Galatians has been called the "Magna Carta of Christian Liberty" and "The Christian Emancipation Proclamation." As in the days of Paul and the Reformation, the book of Galatians still exerts a powerful spiritual influence on the thinking of those who can comprehend its timeless truths.

HISTORICAL SETTING

In the third century BC, Celtic warrior tribes known as Gauls migrated from France to northern Asia Minor (modern-day Turkey). This geographical region became known as Galatia, which simply means "the country of the Gauls." In 25 BC the Roman Empire combined ethnic Galatia with the southern part of Asia Minor to form the new Roman province of Galatia. Because the name Galatia referred to both the geographical area and the Roman province, the exact historical setting of Paul's letter to the Galatians is difficult to determine. A majority of conservative scholars believe Paul wrote to the churches of southern Galatia. If this is the correct interpretation, then the letter would likely have been written in AD 48–49 between the first and second missionary journeys, making Paul's letter to the Galatians his earliest epistle.

Paul and Barnabas were sent out from the church in (Syrian) Antioch to engage in missionary work (Acts 13:1–3). Their first missionary journey took them to Cyprus and southern (provincial) Galatia before they returned to the church at Antioch (Acts 14:26). Paul and Barnabas reported to the church all that God had done through them on their missionary travels (Acts 14:27–28). During their stay at Antioch, some Jewish teachers came from Jerusalem to Galatia and began teaching the Christians that to be saved, the Gentiles must

11

adhere to the Old Testament Mosaic Law (the Law God gave Moses on Mount Sinai) (Acts 15:1–2). Paul and Barnabas disagreed vehemently with these Jewish teachers about the way of salvation (Acts 15:2). When the disagreement could not be resolved in the church at Antioch, Paul, Barnabas, and others went to Jerusalem to settle this important question with the apostles (Acts 15:2–4; Galatians 2:1–10). Even though the apostles agreed that keeping the Law of Moses was not required for salvation or sanctification (Acts 15:6–30), the false teachers continued to teach that man is saved by grace plus works. Paul's letter to the Galatians was a rebuke to the Christians for allowing themselves to be deceived by these false teachers.

SPIRITUAL SIGNIFICANCE

Galatians helps Christians understand the sufficiency of grace for salvation apart from works. Secondly, it exposes the trap believers lay for themselves when they make the Old Testament Law a means of sanctification. The OT Law was the law that God gave Moses on Mount Sinai, which served primarily as Israel's national constitution and instructed them regarding God's expectations for the nation. Thirdly, Paul's castigation of the false teachers should be a rebuke to many New Testament believers who have failed to remain loyal to the gospel of Jesus Christ. In a day of unparalleled ecumenism and religious legalism, Paul's unyielding devotion to Jesus Christ and His gospel is a convicting reminder to some of their misplaced religious loyalties. Finally, the book of Galatians reveals several characteristics of false teachers.

Galatians will challenge you to abandon all forms of religious legalism and encourage you to submit entirely to God's grace for spiritual advancement. The ensuing freedom will not be self-indulgent license but God's liberating power, which will enable you to serve the (only) One who can set man free. In order to remain in this freedom, you'll need to stand firm in this liberty against false teachers (Galatians 5:7–8), stand against your own fleshly desires (Galatians 5:17), and stand against the fallacy that man can be saved or sanctified by anything other than God's grace.

ONE

DON'T MESS WITH THE GOSPEL

Read Introduction, Galatians 1:1–10; other references as given.

Paul begins his letter with a brief greeting (Galatians 1:1–5) and then rebukes the Galatian believers for drifting away from the true gospel. Using some of the strongest words of denunciation in the New Testament, Paul said they had not only left the gospel—they had left Jesus Christ Himself! This lesson reminds believers to stand up for the truth and stand against all attempts to redefine the gospel of God according to man's ideas.

Before you begin, please pray that God would reveal Himself to you through His Word and give you the grace to accept the spiritual truths He will teach you.

Lombardi Time Rule:

If the leader arrives early, he or she has time to pray, prepare the room, and greet others personally.

ADD GROUP INSIGHTS BELOW

1. Irish statesman and philosopher Edmund Burke said, "It is ordained in the eternal constitution of things that men of intemperate minds cannot be free. Their passions forge their chains."

   a. Besides the **Magna Carta of Christian Liberty**, what other title has been given to the book of Galatians (see Introduction)?

   _____

   b. What does the name **Galatia** mean (see Introduction)?

   _____

2. Give a brief summary of the historical setting that prompted the writing of Galatians (see Introduction).

    _____

    _____

    _____

    _____

    _____

3. Several of the New Testament letters, including Galatians, were written to local churches or groups of churches to address specific problems within the assemblies. These epistles, inspired by the Holy Spirit (2 Peter 1:20–21), have provided believers with God's divine instruction throughout the history of the church. Galatians addresses   the problem of false teachers instructing others to do something else besides trusting in Jesus Christ alone to be saved and to grow spiritually.

    a. *Do you think* there is still a problem in the church with false religious teachers adding other things to the doctrine of salvation by grace? Yes / No / Somewhat

    b. If you answered affirmatively to question #3a, what are some things *you think* religious leaders erroneously add to the doctrine of salvation by grace?

        _____

        _____

        _____

        _____

4. The phrase **grace and peace** (Galatians 1:3) is a standard greeting that appears 17 times in the New Testament (NT hereafter). It is, however, more than a standard greeting. God is the source of grace and peace, and His grace is the foundation of the believer's relationship with Him.

a. In all 17 NT occurrences, the word **grace** always appears before **peace** (Galatians 1:3). What *do you think* the specific order of this phrase teaches?

_____

_____

b. Give the meaning and source of each of the two gifts (Galatians 1:3).

_____

_____

_____

_____

Zip-It Rule:

Group members should agree to disagree, but should never be disagreable.

———

ADDITIONAL INSIGHTS

5. Christ's death on the cross was in complete accord with the Father's will (Galatians 1:4). In addition to the provision of eternal salvation (John 3:16), what other reason is given for Christ's death (Galatians 1:4; Titus 2:14)?

_____

_____

_____

6. How were the believers in Galatia (and all Christians) saved (Galatians 1:6)?

_____

_____

7. In the New Testament Paul often identified himself as an apostle (Galatians 1:1) when he wanted to establish apostolic authority in an effort to correct a doctrinal problem.

a. Describe the problem that had arisen in the churches of Galatia (Galatians 1:6–8; 3:1–3; 4:21).

_____

_____

_____

_____

b. Describe these false teachers who were distorting the message of salvation by grace and sanctification (spiritual growth) by grace (Galatians 1:7; 4:17; 6:12–13).

_____

_____

_____

_____

_____

8. a. Many Christians are dangerously tolerant of false teachers within the church. What are some negative results of false teaching (Galatians 1:7; 1 Timothy 1:3–4; 2 Timothy 4:3–4)?

_____

_____

_____

b. Who or what had the Galatian believers deserted (Galatians 1:6)?

_____

9. The word **pervert** (Galatians 1:7; Gk. *metastrepho* — to distort, pervert, to turn around, often into something opposite) is used only three times in the entire Greek NT; Galatians 1:7; Acts 2:20; James 4:9). In both other references the word indicates something being changed in an entirely opposite direction (sun to darkness, laughter into mourning).

a. Using the root definition of the Greek word for **pervert** as a help, explain how the gospel of Jesus Christ was being turned in an opposite (theological) direction by the false teachers.

_____

_____

_____

_____

_____

Want to learn how to disciple another person, lead a life-changing Bible study or start another study? Go to www.Lamplighters USA.org/training to learn how.

b. How did the apostle Paul emphasize that the gospel of Jesus Christ must not be distorted or turned in a different direction (Galatians 1:8–9)?

_____

_____

_____

_____

_____

ADDITIONAL
INSIGHTS

10. Why *do you think* some Christians readily adopt man-made religious rules or regulations rather than accepting God's Word as their final authority and living under grace?

_____

_____

_____

_____

_____

11. a. What would be the result if Paul was more concerned about pleasing man than God (Galatians 1:10)?

_____

b. What *do you think* are some indications that a Christian is more concerned with the approval of man than the approval of God?

_____

_____

c. In what areas of your life, if any, are you more concerned about man's approval (fellow workers, neighbors, family, other Christians, etc.) than pleasing God?

_____

_____

_____

_____

_____

_____

TWO

ONE MESSAGE FOR ALL PEOPLES

Read Galatians 1:11–24; other references as given.

In the first lesson the apostle Paul conveyed a greeting from some unnamed fellow Christians and then rebuked the Galatian believers for deserting Jesus Christ.

In this lesson Paul emphasizes that it was God, not man, who revealed the gospel to him. But had Paul misunderstood God's revelation to him? Paul defended his conversion experience by saying the original apostles confirmed that what he had received (the true gospel) was the same truth they had believed. This lesson emphasizes the essence and the importance of proclaiming the historic gospel—one unaltered by man, not stripped of God's power to transform lives.

Before you begin, please pray that God would reveal Himself to you through His Word and give you the grace to accept the spiritual truths He will teach you.

Volunteer Rule:

If the leader asks for volunteers to read, pray, and answer the questions, group members will be more inclined to invite newcomers.

ADD GROUP INSIGHTS BELOW

1. Paul was an apostle commissioned by God and not man (Galatians 1:1). The gospel he preached wasn't given to him by man; nor did he learn it from man (Galatians 1:11–12). Nowhere else in the New Testament did Paul emphasize these facts to such an extent. Why do you think Paul emphasized this truth so strongly?

    _____

    _____

    _____

2. a. Who does Paul credit for his salvation (Galatians 1:15–16)?

   _____

   b. When you give your personal testimony, are you careful to give glory to God? Note: Your personal testimony is the essential information about how you were born again (saved). If you are not sure what it means to be born again according to the Bible, read the Final Exam located in the back of this study. It will explain how to be born again according to the Bible.

   _____

   _____

3. The Judaistic legalizers who troubled the early churches (including the Galatian churches) were Jewish teachers or Gentiles who converted to Judaism and now believed that adherence to the OT Mosaic Law was mandatory for both the salvation and sanctification of Christians. They used their identification or association with the church in Jerusalem (Acts 15:1, 24) and "letters of commendation" (2 Corinthians 3:1) as their credentials in an effort to control and manipulate the thinking of these new Galatian believers.

   a. Have you ever noticed a religious leader or layperson exercising a form of spiritual control over others? Can you give an example? Be careful not to mention specific names or denominations.

   _____

   _____

   _____

   b. What are some methods that religious parasites often use to control others?

   _____

   _____

_____

_____

4. a. In what ways do you think Paul's explanation of his former life in Judaism (Galatians 1:14–17) helped the Galatian Christians understand the truth?

_____

_____

_____

b. Instead of boasting about his relationship with the church in Jerusalem, Paul de-emphasized his association with it (Galatians 1:15–19). In light of the present problem in the churches of Galatia, why do you think he would do this?

_____

_____

_____

5. a. Why did God reveal Jesus Christ to Paul (Galatians 1:16)?

_____

_____

b. If you are saved (born again), why do you think God revealed Jesus Christ to you? Be as complete as possible with your answer.

_____

_____

_____

6. An individual's religious training prior to salvation can be a tremendous help (2 Timothy 3:15–16), or it can be a great hindrance to his or her spiritual growth. In the case

59:59 Rule:

Participants appreciate when the leader starts and finishes the studies on time—all in one hour (the 59:59 rule). If the leader doesn't complete the entire lesson, the participants will be less likely to do their weekly lessons and the Bible study discussion will tend to wander.

———

ADDITIONAL INSIGHTS

of the Jewish legalizers, their prior religious training was a stumbling block to them, hindering their understanding and acceptance of the sufficiency of God's grace.

a. What things were you taught prior to salvation that were in conflict with God's Word? Be careful not to mention specific denominations.

_____

_____

_____

_____

b. What advice would you give a younger Christian who is struggling with what the Bible clearly teaches versus the man-made religious traditions he or she was taught that are contrary to God's Word?

_____

_____

_____

_____

_____

7. Compare the results of the false teachers (Galatians 1:7) and those from the ministry of the apostle Paul (Galatians 1:21–24).

_____

_____

_____

_____

8. Galatians 2:1–10 explains some of the details of a visit made by Paul, Barnabas, and others to the church in Jerusalem. Their visit to the Jerusalem church initiated a church council

commonly known as the *Jerusalem Council* (Acts 15:4–31).

a. Why did Paul, Barnabas, and others go up to Jerusalem to the Jerusalem Council (Acts 15:1–2)?

_____

_____

_____

_____

b. How did Paul and Barnabas respond to the false teachers who were saying that the Gentiles (non-Jews) must be circumcised in order to be saved (Acts 15:2)?

_____

_____

9. When was the last time you stood up for the truth in the face of opposition? What were the circumstances, and what was the outcome?

_____

_____

_____

_____

_____

ADDITIONAL INSIGHTS

THREE

AVOID LEGALISM

Read Galatians 2:1–21;
other references as given.

The true gospel is the revelation of Jesus Christ to an individual (Galatians 1:12) that is offered freely as a benevolent act of the sovereign grace of God. Man's salvation is based entirely upon God's grace apart from man's works (Galatians 1:15).

In this lesson Paul defends his refusal to circumcise a Gentile believer (a fellow missionary named Titus) according to Jewish law, to prove that his (Paul's) commitment to the true gospel was consistent throughout his missionary work. If Paul had allowed Titus to be circumcised, it would prove to the Jews that keeping the Old Testament Law of Moses was necessary for Gentiles (non-Jews) to be saved. Paul's refusal to circumcise Titus supports the teaching that salvation is by grace alone through faith alone.

Before you begin, please pray that God would reveal Himself to you through His Word and give you the grace to accept the spiritual truths He will teach you.

Focus Rule:

If the leader helps the group members focus on the Bible, they will gain confidence to study God's Word on their own.

ADD GROUP INSIGHTS BELOW

1. Paul said the gospel he preached was authentic because it was a revelation from Jesus Christ (Galatians 1:11–12). In Jerusalem, however, Paul met privately with the leaders (Galatians 2:2, **those who were of reputation**) and submitted the message (gospel) he preached privately. Why do you think Paul did this privately?

_____

_____

_____

_____

2. Titus accompanied Paul to Jerusalem, most likely as living proof that a person can be saved without submitting to the Mosaic Law (circumcision was the rite or symbol that a person had adopted the OT Law).

    a. Why was it important for Titus not to submit to the rite of circumcision (Galatians 2:3–5)?

        _____

        _____

        _____

    b. What do you think is the meaning of the phrase **that the truth of the gospel might continue with you** (Galatians 2:5)?

        _____

        _____

        _____

        _____

3. What do you think is the meaning of the phrase **those who were of reputation contributed nothing to me** (Galatians 2:6 NASB)?

    _____

    _____

4. Instead of rejecting Paul's message of salvation by grace, the church leaders in Jerusalem endorsed his ministry (Galatians 2:7–10). They realized God had given Peter and Paul the same gospel message, but they had been given distinctive

ministries. Peter was to go to the Jews (circumcised) and Paul to the Gentiles.

a. Galatians 2:7–10 teaches us some important principles about ministry and working together for the cause of Christ. Name at least three.

_____

_____

_____

_____

b. Who did the church leaders ask Paul to remember (Galatians 2:10)?

_____

In what ways do you personally fulfill this important responsibility?

_____

_____

_____

5. After Paul returned from Jerusalem to Antioch, Peter visited the church at Antioch (Galatians 2:11). During this visit Paul confronted Peter over his sinful conduct.

a. What did Peter do that caused Paul to confront him (Galatians 2:11–12)?

_____

_____

_____

_____

_____

_____

If the leader asks all the study questions, the group discussion will be more likely to stay on track.

ADDITIONAL INSIGHTS

b. Why did Peter do this when he knew God had already accepted the Gentiles (Galatians 2:12)?

_____

_____

c. What were the results of Peter's actions (Galatians 2:12–13)?

_____

_____

_____

6. If a Christian brother or sister continues in sin, the Scriptures instruct Christians to go privately in an effort to restore the sinning believer (Matthew 18:15; Galatians 6:1). Why do you think it was necessary for Paul to confront Peter in public (Galatians 2:14, **before them all**)?

_____

_____

_____

_____

_____

7. According to some religious teachers, man's salvation must be secured by keeping a moral code or set of religious laws. What two statements does Paul make to disprove this teaching that man can be saved by works (Galatians 2:16)?

_____

_____

_____

8. a. When a believer sins after he has been justified by faith in Christ, is Jesus Christ the one who made him sin (Galatians 2:17)? _____

b. If man could acquire righteousness before God by means of the Law, then what would also be true (Galatians 2:21)?

_____

_____

9. There is a very important spiritual truth about the Christian life in Galatians 2:20. What is it?

_____

_____

_____

_____

_____

_____

10. Many Christians say they want to live for God. While this statement is not scripturally wrong (Galatians 2:19; 1 Thessalonians 4:1, 7), there is a big difference in living for God and the biblical truth being taught in Galatians 2:20. What do you think is the difference between Christians "living for God" and realizing they were crucified with Christ (at salvation) and that it is no longer they who live, but it is Christ living through them?

_____

_____

_____

_____

Has your group become a "Holy huddle?" Learn how to reach out to others by taking online leadership training.

ADDITIONAL INSIGHTS

ADDITIONAL INSIGHTS

Four

SONS OF ABRAHAM

**Read Galatians 3:1–14;
other references as given.**

Does a Christian become spiritually mature by obeying a set of religious rules or by learning to live by grace? In Galatians 3 Paul answers this question logically (vs. 1-5), historically (the example of Abraham, vs. 6–18), and theologically (the origin and purpose of the Law, vs. 19-29).

Paul uses some of the most confrontational language directed at believers found anywhere in the New Testament (Galatians 3:1, **O foolish Galatians**). Rather than appealing to them as believers, Paul equates them with secular Roman citizens (devoid of the Spirit) to help them grasp their spiritual blindness and turn them back to Christ.

Before you begin, please pray that God would reveal Himself to you through His Word and give you the grace to accept the spiritual truths you will be learning.

1. What words and phrases does the apostle Paul use to gain the attention of his readers and alert them to the seriousness of their error (Galatians 3:1–3)?

    _____

    _____

    _____

    _____

Gospel Gold Rule:

Try to get all the answers to the questions—not just the easy ones. Go for the gold.

———

ADD GROUP
INSIGHTS BELOW

2. The words **foolish** (Gk. *anoetos*—foolish, without thinking, thoughtless, unreflecting) and **bewitched** (Gk. *ebaskanen*—bewitch, cast a spell upon, bring a person to damage through an evil eye or spoken word) are very strong words. Interestingly, Paul's use of the word **foolish** is not a violation of Christ's prohibition in Matthew 5:22 because it is an entirely different Greek word.

    a. The problem in the churches of Galatia is presented in the form of two questions (Galatians 3:3, 5). In your own words, describe the problem in the churches that resulted in some of the strongest words of rebuke in the entire New Testament. Be as clear as possible with your answer.

    _____

    _____

    _____

    b. Using the two definitions stated above, describe in your own words what happens to believers when they allow false teaching to influence them.

    _____

    _____

    _____

3. The churches of Galatia were established on Paul's first missionary journey several years after the crucifixion of Christ (Acts 13:4–14:26).

    a. What do you think is meant by the phrase **Jesus Christ was clearly portrayed among you as crucified** (Galatians 3:1)?

    _____

    _____

    _____

b. If you were to answer the question in Galatians 3:2, what would you say?

_____

_____

c. Restate the second question in Galatians 3:3 in your own words. Be complete with your answer to make sure you grasp the truth being taught in the form of a question.

_____

_____

_____

d. What is the correct answer to the question asked in Galatians 3:5?

_____

_____

_____

4. If a Christian doesn't become spiritually mature by attempting to keep the keep the Law, how do you think a believer becomes spiritually mature?

_____

_____

_____

_____

5. Besides the influence of the false teachers, what is another reason the Galatian believers deserted God (Galatians 3:4)?

_____

_____

Want to learn how to disciple another person, lead a life-changing Bible study or start another study? Go to www.Lamplighters USA.org/training to learn how.

ADDITIONAL INSIGHTS

_____

_____

_____

_____

6. The Galatian Christians were not saved by keeping the Law (Galatians 3:5). Even Abraham, the Old Testament patriarch, the man to whom the Judaizers paid much homage (respect, honor), was not saved by the Law (Galatians 3:6; Romans 4:2). Besides the "friend of God" (James 2:23), what else is Abraham called (Galatians 3:9)?

_____

7. a. If a Christian places himself under the OT Law as a means of obtaining salvation, under what does he also place himself if he is not able to keep the entire Law (Galatians 3:10)?

_____

b. Now examine your life closely. Are you trusting in Jesus Christ alone for eternal life, or are you "trusting" in Jesus Christ plus something else for salvation (good works, church membership, baptism, the Golden Rule, a meaningful religious experience, sacraments, a general belief in God, etc.)?

_____

_____

_____

_____

_____

_____

_____

_____

8. Galatians 3:13–14 present a beautiful picture of Christ's complete work of redemption. Give at least four important truths taught in these verses.

_____

_____

_____

_____

_____

Did you know Lamplighters is more than a small group ministry? It is a discipleship training ministry that uses a small group format to train disciple-makers. If every group trained one person per study, God would use these new disciple-makers to reach more people for Christ.

ADDITIONAL INSIGHTS

ADDITIONAL INSIGHTS

FIVE

THE PURPOSE OF THE LAW

Read Galatians 3:15–29;
other references as given.

The believer's ongoing relationship to the Old Testament Law of Moses is a critical question that every Christian must resolve if he expects to live for Christ.

Is the ultimate purpose of the Law fulfilled when we come to Christ, making it obsolete in the lives of believers, or does it continue to serve as a standard of conduct for the believer and reflection of the moral will of God? Is the believer obligated to keep the Ten Commandments but not the rest of the Law? Does the Law somehow aid the spiritual growth of the believer? These are critical questions for every serious follower of Christ, and Galatians 3 provides definitive answers to these ageless questions.

Before you begin, please pray that God would reveal Himself to you through His Word and give you the grace to accept the spiritual truths you will be learning.

1. The believer's relationship to the Law is illustrated by a human covenant or will (Galatians 3:15–17). In Abraham's time, a covenant involving two parties was generally confirmed by a ceremony in which an animal was divided into two parts and the parties exchanged promises as they stood between the parts of the animal (Genesis 15:9–12). In the Abrahamic covenant (Genesis 12:1–4; 13:14–17; 15:1–7; 17:1–8), God promised to establish an everlasting covenant with Abraham

No-Trespassing Rule:

To keep the Bible study on track, avoid talking about political parties, church denominations, and Bible translations.

ADD GROUP
INSIGHTS BELOW

and make him a father to a multitude of nations (Genesis 17:5).

a. How did God fulfill His promise to Abraham (Galatians 3:16)?

_____

b. What did not invalidate God's promise to Abraham (Galatians 3:17)?

_____

_____

2. An element of God's original promise or covenant to Abraham is fulfilled when people from every nation turn to Christ and are saved (Romans 4:16–17). What does the continuing fulfillment of this promise teach about God's character?

_____

_____

_____

3. Galatians 3:19–25 is the most definitive passage in the New Testament that addresses the question of the original and continuing purpose of the Old Testament Law. Paul introduces this section with two more unvoiced questions; (1) If the Law is not the source of salvation (Galatians 3:5–6) or sanctification (Galatians 3:3), why was it ever given (Galatians 3:19)?—and, (2) Does the Law contradict the promises of God (Galatians 3:21, *author's paraphrase*)?

a. There are two important truths about the Law taught in Galatians 3:19. What are they?

_____

_____

_____

_____

_____

_____

b. Paul said the Law continued **till the Seed should come to whom the promise was made** (Galatians 3:19). What does this mean (Galatians 3:16)? Who is the Seed?

_____

_____

_____

_____

If you use table tents or name tags, it will help visitors feel more comfortable and new members will be assimilated more easily into your group.

———

ADDITIONAL INSIGHTS

4. The word **tutor** (Galatians 3:24–25; Gk. *paidagogos*—child custodian or attendant) was a male nursemaid employed by wealthy Roman or Grecian families to provide general oversight of a boy between the ages of six and sixteen. The responsibility of the male nursemaid ceased when the boy became an official son, an act of unconditional acceptance by the father through the formal rite of adoption.

a. In this illustration, rich in cultural meaning, who is the **tutor** or male nursemaid (Galatians 3:24–25)?

_____

b. In ancient Rome and Greece the male nursemaid handed the boy over to the custody of the father. Who are believers handed over to when they are saved (Galatians 3:26)? Be clear as possible with your answer.

_____

c. What continuing responsibility did the tutor have after the son was adopted by the father?

_____

d. If a boy was adopted by his father, given the status of an official son, and made an heir to the family's wealth, do you think he would want to return to the authority of his male nursemaid? _____

Why? _____

_____

_____

_____

_____

5. If an individual places his faith in the finished work of Christ and accepts the free gift of salvation, is he still obligated to keep any portion of the OT Law (Galatians 3:24–25; 4:4–5; Romans 6:14; 10:4)?

    _____

    _____

    _____

    _____

    How sure are you of your answer?
    10% / 25% / 50% / 75% / 100%

6. If the Law is not a means of salvation or sanctification, what purpose, if any, does it still serve (Galatians 3:22–24; 1 Timothy 1:8–10)?

    _____

    _____

    _____

    _____

    _____

7. a. What is the correct *legal* title for a person who has trusted Christ (Galatians 3:26)?

        _____

b. Besides the answer you gave in # 7a, name three things that happen to a person when he/she accepts Christ by faith (Galatians 3:26–29).

_____

_____

_____

_____

8. Some Christians believe that women can serve in pastoral leadership positions over men, and others believe the pastoral office is restricted only to men. According to the advocates of the first perspective, passages that address the biblical qualifications for spiritual leadership (1 Timothy 3:1–10, 12–13; Titus 1:5–9) are considered culturally bound and not applicable today. Although they believe that the qualifications for spiritual leadership still apply, they believe the references to the male gender should be understood generically. They offer Galatians 3:28 as biblical support for the inclusion of women in the role of pastoral leadership. Do you agree with this interpretation? _____

Why? (Note: support your answer with biblical reasoning.)

_____

_____

_____

_____

_____

_____

_____

Use the side margins to write down spiritual insights from other people in your group. Add the person's name and the date to help you remember in the future.

———

ADDITIONAL INSIGHTS

ADDITIONAL INSIGHTS

Six

Sons or Slaves?

Read Galatians 4:1–11; other references as given.

If a Christian doesn't understand the relationship between law and grace, he'll be tempted to fall prey to legalism. Legalism is man's attempt to gain acceptance with God and live for God in the power of the flesh. Legalism leads individuals away from God (because it focuses on human effort rather than faith in God) while it gives them a false sense of spiritual advancement. The motive is right (desire for spiritual advancement), but the method (sanctification through the Law or works) is wrong.

In Galatians 4 Paul explains spiritual adoption (vs. 1–7), laments the Galatians' spiritual regression (vs. 8–11), seeks their repentance (vs.12–20), and challenges their spiritual reasoning (Galatians 4:21–5:1).

Before you begin, please pray that God would reveal Himself to you through His Word and give you the grace to accept the spiritual truths you will be learning.

Transformation Rule:

Seek for personal transformation, not mere information, from God's Word.

ADD GROUP INSIGHTS BELOW

1. While a Jewish boy was granted adult status at age twelve and a Grecian boy at age eighteen, a Roman boy was officially adopted at the age appointed by the father. The Roman father acknowledged his male child as his son and legal heir at a sacred festival known as a *Liberalia*. During this festival the son received his *toga virilis* (the garment of adulthood) and discarded the *toga praetexta* (the garment of youth). Never again would the son be considered a child.

43

a. What are the similarities and differences between a slave and a Roman child who had not yet been adopted by his father (Galatians 4:1–2)?

_____

_____

_____

_____

_____

_____

_____

b. In other passages of Scripture the words **child** or **children** are used to describe; a person of youthful age (Mark 12:19), a believer in Jesus Christ (John 1:12) and spiritual offspring (1 Corinthians 4:17; Titus 1:4). Do any of the definitions listed above apply to the word **children** (Galatians 4:3), or does the word mean something different (Galatians 4:3–5)?

_____

_____

2. There are four important things stated about Jesus Christ in Galatians 4:4. What are they?

_____

_____

_____

_____

_____

_____

3. What do you think is meant by the phrase **the fullness of the time** (Galatians 4:4)?

_____

_____

_____

Would you like to learn how to prepare a life-changing Bible study using a simple 4-step process? Contact Lamplighters and ask about ST-A-R-T.

ADDITIONAL INSIGHTS

4. The phrase **born under the law** (Galatians 4:4) tells us much about the ministry of Jesus and how to interpret the gospels correctly.

   a. What does the phrase **born under the law** mean?

   _____

   _____

   b. How should the fact that Christ was **born under the [OT] law** influence or affect a Christian's interpretation of the gospels?

   _____

   _____

   _____

   _____

5. Interestingly, the word **redeem** (Galatians 4:5; Gk. *exiagoradzo*—to redeem, to buy out of the marketplace) is used instead of words such as *justify*, *reconcile*, or *save*.

   a. What price was paid to redeem man from the curse of the Law (1 Peter 1:18–19)?

   _____

   b. When man receives God's gift of salvation (Romans 10:13), what three things does he receive (Galatians 4:5–7)?

   _____

   _____

45

6. a. When a person receives Jesus Christ as Savior, he is adopted into God's family and becomes a legal son of God (Galatians 4:5–6). How do the Scriptures describe man prior to the time of salvation (Ephesians 2:2–3)?

_____

_____

b. What five negative results does man experience as a result of not receiving the adoption as sons (Ephesians 2:12)?

_____

_____

_____

_____

_____

c. If you are a Christian, what are you doing to help others escape the wrath of God?

_____

_____

_____

_____

7. In ancient times Jews exhibited such great respect for the name of God (Yahweh/Jehovah) that they would not even say His name aloud. In the work of translation, Jewish scribes would use a new pen every time they wrote the name of God. Now as legal sons of God, Christians are encouraged to address God as Father (Matthew 6:9; Note: Abba is the Aramaic diminutive for "father," perhaps equivalent to the English word *daddy* or *papa*). What areas of the Christian experience should be affected by this invitation to spiritual intimacy?

_____

_____

_____

_____

_____

8. a. Restate the question in Galatians 4:9 in your own words.

_____

_____

_____

If the leader places a watch on the table, participants will feel confident that the Bible study will be completed on time. If the leader doesn't complete the lesson each week, participants will be less likely to do their weekly lessons, and the discussion will not be as rich.

————

ADDITIONAL INSIGHTS

b. What are the **weak and beggarly elements** that the Galatians had returned (Galatians 4:9–10)?

_____

_____

_____

c. Why do you think the Bible uses these descriptive words to describe them?

_____

_____

_____

_____

ADDITIONAL INSIGHTS

SEVEN

PROMISES, PROMISES

Read Galatians 4:12–31; other references as given.

In this lesson Paul uses a familiar Old Testament story of two sons, Ishmael and Isaac, to illustrate the believer's struggle of trying to live for God by law and grace at the same time. In the illustration, Ishmael, born to Abraham and his female servant Hagar, represents living by the flesh. Isaac, born later to Abraham and Sarah, represents living by grace. As the children grew, jealous conflict between the two families boiled over to the point that Hagar and her son, Ishmael, eventually left. Paul's point: A believer cannot live comfortably by law (legalism) and grace—one has to go!

Before you begin, please pray that God would reveal Himself to you through His Word and give you the grace to accept the spiritual truths you will be learning.

Drawing Rule:

To learn how to draw everyone into the group discussion without calling on anyone, go to www.Lamplighters USA.org/training.

———

ADD GROUP
INSIGHTS BELOW

1. What was Paul fearful of if the Galatians continued in their present spiritual direction (Galatians 4:9–12)?

    _____

    _____

2. a. Paul's love for the Galatians and concern for their spiritual condition is clearly evident. List several words and phrases he uses to express the depth of his love for these believers (Galatians 4:12–20).

    _____

_____

_____

_____

_____

b. In what specific ways are you communicating love and spiritual concern to fellow believers?

_____

_____

_____

_____

3. When the believer ceases to function by grace and returns to law for sanctification, he inevitably loses something very important. What does he lose (Galatians 4:15)?

_____

_____

_____

4. Paul returns to the subject of the false teachers and gives another characteristic of their ministries (Galatians 4:17).

a. What do you think is the meaning of the phrase **they want to exclude you, that you may be zealous for them** (Galatians 4:17)?

_____

_____

_____

_____

b. What methods, ploys, or tactics (if any) have you noticed false teachers using to cause their followers to seek them?

_____

_____

5. Paul confronted the Galatians and false teachers with their lack of understanding of the Hebrew Scriptures (Galatians 4:21–5:1). He uses the story of Isaac and Ishmael (Genesis 16:1–16; 21:1–13) to prove that Christians are not under the Law. Paul's assignment of a deeper meaning (in this case, spiritual) to the historical facts is often called *allegorizing* (Galatians 4:24; an example of an allegory is John Bunyan's book *A Pilgrim's Progress*). Do you think Christians should look for an allegorical or hidden meaning as he or she studies the Bible?

    Always / Sometimes / Never

    Why? Explain your answer.

    _____

    _____

    _____

    _____

6. The two women, Hagar and Sarah, represent two covenants or promises from God. From their wombs came two children who became patriarchs of great nations (Genesis 17:16; 21:13). The birth of Ishmael represents the first or natural birth, and the birth of Isaac represents the second or supernatural birth.

    a. Hagar represents the giving of the Law at Mount Sinai in Arabia (Galatians 4:25). What is the result of the first or natural birth (Galatians 4:24–25)?

       _____

       _____

    b. When the Law was given, the children of Israel displayed an attitude that is characteristic of all believers who live under law instead of grace. What is this attitude, and

51

what is its result (Exodus 19:14–16; Galatians 4:15a [first portion of the verse])?

_____

_____

7. a. If you are a Christian, does God expect you to live as a child of the bondwoman or as a child of promise (Galatians 4:28)?

_____

Why? _____

_____

_____

_____

b. What evidence do you (and others) see in your life that you are living by grace (by the power of the Holy Spirit) as a child of promise?

_____

_____

_____

8. In the Genesis account of Ishmael and Isaac, hostility became so intense between them that they could not live together (Genesis 21:8–14). The original resolution of this difficult situation helps believers understand an important principle of spiritual development. What is this principle (Galatians 4:30)?

_____

_____

_____

_____

EIGHT

LIBERTY OR LICENSE?

Read Galatians 5:1–15;
other references as given.

If Christian lives by grace totally apart from the law, won't they be tempted to turn this liberty into a license to sin? Not if they allow themselves to be controlled by the Holy Spirit. Only through the Spirit's control can a believer gain true victory over the sinful nature.

In this lesson Paul begins to teach his readers how to live by grace. He encourages the Galatian believers to live boldly in God's grace and to refuse to be hindered by false teachers who say spiritual progress occurs by keeping man-made religious rules.

Before you begin, please pray that God would reveal Himself to you through His Word and give you the grace to accept the spiritual truths you will be learning.

Balance Rule:

To learn how to balance the group discussion, go to www.Lamplighters USA.org/training or call 800 507- 9516.

———

ADD GROUP INSIGHTS BELOW

1. Besides being the theme verse of Paul's letter, Galatians 5:1 also serves as the conclusion to the preceding section (Galatians 3:1–4:31) and the introduction to the third major section of the book (Galatians 5:2–6:18). Christ's sacrifice on the cross provided believers with salvation from eternal judgment and freedom (Galatians 5:1). As you reflect upon the development of Paul's argument to this point in the letter, what is the specific meaning of the word **liberty** in Galatians 5:1?

_____

_____

_____

_____

2. While Christ has provided freedom for all believers, the continuing responsibility of keeping this freedom rests upon the individual Christian (Galatians 5:1).

    a. State in your own words two things every Christian must do in order to safeguard the freedom Christ has provided.

        _____

        _____

        _____

    b. Take a minute to do a personal spiritual inventory. Do you honestly believe that you are free from all forms of legalism?

        _____

        _____

    c. One way to examine whether you are free from all forms of legalism is to evaluate why you seek to obey God. What is the primary reason you live for God?

        _____

        _____

3. Many in the Galatian churches had been deceived by the Judaizers (Galatians 1:6; 3:1–3). Others, who had not yet fallen prey to the Judaizers (notice the word _if_ in Galatians 5:2), were still uncertain about their relationship to the Law. What two warnings does Paul give all believers who are thinking about placing themselves under the Law (Galatians 5:2–3)?

    _____

    _____

_____

_____

4. At first glance the sobering phrases **estranged from Christ** and **fallen from grace** (Galatians 5:4) appear to teach that it is possible for believers to lose their salvation.

   a. To whom is Paul speaking (Galatians 5:4)?

   _____

   _____

   b. What important spiritual truth does the Bible teach in Galatians 5:3–4?

   _____

   _____

   _____

   _____

5. While the Galatian believers were saved by grace and had initially lived by grace, they had now turned away from this truth (Galatians 5:7). In Galatians 5:7–11, there are four important reasons why some Christians fall into doctrinal error. What are they?

   1. _____

      _____ (v. _____)

   2. _____

      _____ (v. _____)

   3. _____

      _____ (v. _____)

   4. _____

      _____ (v. _____)

6. Christians should not abuse the freedom Christ has given them by using their **liberty as an opportunity for the flesh** (Galatians 5:13). What does this mean?

_____

_____

7. Some Christians are quick to justify their questionable or worldly actions by saying they are exercising their personal liberty in Christ. Mary Lou Cummins said, "When we refuse to consciously and deliberately choose specific behaviors, the powerful ocean of society that we live in is ready to wash us out to sea. There we can bob helplessly along with the crowd."

   a. How can a Christian be sure that he is not turning his liberty in Christ into a license to sin (Galatians 5:13)?

   _____

   _____

   _____

   b. What do the Scriptures teach about a believer who exercises his personal liberty in Christ even though he knows his actions are causing another brother or sister to stumble (1 Corinthians 8:10–13)? Make your answer as complete as possible.

   _____

   _____

   _____

   _____

8. a. Is there anything in your life that could cause another Christian to stumble in his or her walk with Christ— things that you are excusing by rationalizing that you are simply exercising your personal freedom in Christ?

_____

_____

_____

_____

It's a good time to begin praying and inviting new people for your next Open House.

_____

ADDITIONAL
INSIGHTS

b. If there are things in your life that you are justifying, how might these things impede someone else's walk with Christ or hinder a non-Christian from coming to Christ?

_____

_____

_____

9. a. How can a Christian fulfill the Law (Galatians 5:14)?

_____

_____

b. Give several practical ways you are currently fulfilling this command.

_____

_____

_____

_____

10. Paul has already said that believers experience a loss of joy or blessing when they cease to live by grace (Galatians 4:15). What is another negative by-product of legalistic Christian living (Galatians 5:15)?

_____

_____

_____

ADDITIONAL INSIGHTS

NINE

WALKING IN THE SPIRIT

Read Galatians 5:16–26; other references as given.

The key to living a victorious Christian life is learning to walk in the Spirit. The apostle Paul said, **I say then: Walk in the Spirit, and you shall not fulfill the lust of the flesh**. (Galatians 5:16). What an amazing promise!

But what does it mean to "walk in the Spirit"? Certainly it's not some self-proclaimed announcement by a Christian whose life is marked by the deeds of the flesh. In this lesson you will learn what it means to live by grace and walk in the Spirit.

Before you begin, please pray that God would reveal Himself to you through His Word and give you the grace to accept the spiritual truths you will be learning.

Is your study going well? Consider starting a new group. To learn how, go to www. Lamplighters USA.org/training.

ADD GROUP INSIGHTS BELOW

1. The Bible uses the word **walk** (Gk. *peripateo*—to walk about, to conduct one's life) to emphasize an important principle about the Christian's relationship to God. What is this?

    _____

    _____

    _____

    _____

2. In Paul's letter to the Ephesians, he linked the word **walk** with five important spiritual responsibilities to teach the Ephesian believers (and us) how to walk in the Spirit and

how to experience close communion with their heavenly Father. List these five responsibilities of the Christian life (Ephesians 4:1, 17; 5:2, 8, 15).

1. _____

_____

2. _____

_____

3. _____

_____

4. _____

_____

5. _____

_____

3. What do you think it means to **walk in the Spirit** (Galatians 5:16)?

_____

_____

_____

_____

_____

4. Galatians is a book of contrasts: Paul and the Judaizers, law and grace, faith and works, sons and slaves, Ishmael and Isaac. This is not a coincidence. Galatians teaches us that there are two different paths for the believer—walking in the Spirit and walking in the flesh. Two paths with two entirely different results. Believers live with an internal conflict between these two paths. Choosing the wrong one hinders their walk with God and diminishes their witness for Christ (Galatians 5:17). This war within the soul must be fought in the power of the Holy Spirit if the believer is going

to consistently manifest the fruit of the Spirit (Galatians 5:16–18, 22–23).

a. List the deeds of the flesh (Galatians 5:19–21).

_____

_____

_____

b. What phrase indicates this list is not complete (Galatians 5:21)?

_____

It's time to choose your next study. Turn to the back of the study guide for a list of available studies or go online for the latest studies.

———

ADDITIONAL INSIGHTS

5. In Galatians 5:19 the words **adultery** (sexual relations of married people outside the marriage bond) and **fornication** (sexual relations of unmarried people) are translations of a single Greek word (*porneia*), which can mean both adultery and fornication. The English word *pornography* (*porneia* + *grapho*, to write) comes from this same Greek word.

a. What are some things Satan uses in our society to promote immorality, impurity, and sensuality?

_____

_____

b. What have you done to protect yourself against physical and mental impurity?

_____

_____

_____

_____

6. a. When most people think of idolatry, they visualize a distant land filled with pagan idols of wood and stone. What word does Paul equate with idolatry that dispels

this myth that idolatry is merely something physical (Colossians 3:5)?

_____

b. Now that you know that coveteousness (NIV: "greed") is idolatry (Colossians 3:5), is there anything in your life that you covet (either something you possess or something you would like to have) that could truly be called an idol in your life?

_____

_____

_____

c. What do you think God wants you to do to be released from this idol?

_____

_____

_____

7. Give a brief definition of each of the following terms in Galatians 5:20–21:

1. Sorcery: _____

_____

2. Contentions: _____

_____

3. Jealousies: _____

_____

4. Dissensions: _____

_____

5. Factions (NIV): _____

_____

6. Envy: _____

_____

    Is your life free from these things? Yes / No

_____

Is it time for you to move from being a perpetual learner to a disciple-maker?

ADDITIONAL
INSIGHTS

8. The Bible says anyone who **practices** these things (Galatians 5:19–21) will not inherit the kingdom of God (Galatians 5:21). Paul is talking about not the act of sin but the habit of sin. If a person continues in sinful conduct, does not see anything wrong with his behavior, and possesses no power to change, what does this indicate (1 John 2:3–4; 5:4)?

_____

_____

9. Why do you think the Holy Spirit would direct Paul to use the word **fruit** instead of *deeds* in the phrase **fruit of the Spirit** (Galatians 5:22)?

_____

_____

_____

_____

10. If you have been saved, how are you to live for God (Galatians 5:25)?

_____

_____

_____

_____

_____

_____

_____

ADDITIONAL INSIGHTS

TEN

LIVING BY GRACE

Read Galatians 6:1–7;
other references as given.

How can a Christian know for sure if he is living by grace? The answer is amazingly simple. Is the believer's relationship with others characterized by the fruit of the Spirit or by the deeds of the flesh? Is he investing in the eternal or the temporal?

In Galatians 6 Paul gives specific instruction regarding the believer's relationship to other people (vs. 1–5), financial stewardship (vs. 6–10) and personal sacrifice for Christ (vs. 11–18).

Before you begin, please pray that God would reveal Himself to you through His Word and give you the grace to accept the spiritual truths you will be learning.

1. The word **brethren** (Gk. *adelphoi*) is a term of endearment and an indicator of the depth of spiritual unity that should exist between members of the body of Christ. Besides the word **brethren,** what other encouraging words or phrases are used to describe the Galatian believers (Galatians 3:26, 29; 4:19, 28)?

   _____

   _____

2. The pastors or elders of a particular church have been given the responsibility of providing spiritual oversight for the church (Acts 20:28–32; 1 Timothy 1:3–7). Besides the

Many groups study the Final Exam the week after the final lesson for three reasons: (1) someone might come to Christ, (2) believers gain assurance of salvation, (3) group members learn how to share the gospel.

ADD GROUP
INSIGHTS BELOW

pastors or elders, who else has God ordained to help ensure the spiritual well-being of His people (Galatians 6:1)?

_____

_____

_____

3. The word **overtaken** (Gk. *prolambano*—to overtake by surprise, to overpower before one can escape) indicates the person entered into sin unintentionally (Galatians 6:1). How should the meaning of this particular Greek word affect a Christian's response to an erring believer?

_____

_____

_____

4. a. What are the Christian's biblical responsibilities when he becomes aware that a fellow believer is living in sin (Galatians 6:1)?

_____

_____

_____

b. Some believers have never been taught their biblical responsibility to other members of the body of Christ. Others are familiar with the biblical teaching on this subject but are unwilling to obey God in this area. It has been said that truth is not only violated by falsehood, it may be equally outraged by silence. What are some ungodly ways believers respond to the knowledge of sin in the lives of other Christians (Proverbs 10:17; 16:28; 1 Timothy 5:13)?

_____

_____

_____

c. Do you know a brother or sister in Christ who needs to be restored to spiritual health? If you do, what could you do to help restore him or her to spiritual health?

_____

_____

_____

5. The word **restore** (Gk. *katartidzo*—to restore, to correct, to set in place) was used in secular Greek to describe the medical procedure of setting a broken bone. How should the use of this specific Greek word influence the believer's approach toward a sinning brother or sister?

_____

_____

_____

_____

6. At first glance there appear to be conflicting truths in Galatians 6:2, 5. However, two entirely different Greek words are used for **burden** (Galatians 6:2) and **load** (Galatians 6:5). The word **burden** (Gk. *bare*) is an excessive burden too heavy for a man to bear, and the word **load** (Gk. *phortion*) is a military backpack or soldier's kit. Using the Greek definitions of these two words as a help, explain the two responsibilities every believer should assume within the body of Christ (Galatians 6:2, 5).

_____

_____

_____

_____

7. When the believer lives by grace, he fulfills the law of Christ (Galatians 6:2, 1 Corinthians 9:21). He allows every aspect of his life to be controlled by the Holy Spirit and the love of

For more discipleship help, sign up to receive the Disciple-Maker Tips—a bi-monthly email that provides insights to help your small group function more effectively.

———

ADDITIONAL INSIGHTS

Christ. Besides being called the law of Christ, what else is this law called (Romans 8:2; James 2:8, 12)?

_____

_____

8. Besides the fundamental doctrinal differences between legalism and grace (Galatians 1:6–8; 3:3), there is a major difference in attitude toward sinning brethren. The legalist believes the only reason others fall into sin is because they are not willing to accept the "yoke of the Law." The legalist believes he is incapable of committing such a sin, so his heart is filled with pride and condemnation. What words would you use to describe the attitude every believer should have toward other believers who are caught in sin (Galatians 6:1–5)?

_____

_____

9. In addition to allowing the Spirit to control his relationships with others, the believer should allow the Holy Spirit to control his use of money (Galatians 6:6–10). Although application of this passage extends far beyond financial stewardship, the passage deals specifically with the believer's relationship to money (Note: the beginning words **for, and, therefore** (Galatians 6:8–10) and the phrase **do good to all** (Galatians 6:10), a euphemism for giving alms, support this conclusion).

   a. Restate the commandment in Galatians 6:6 in your own words.

   _____

   _____

   _____

   b. It is significant that the word **share** (Gk. *koinoneo*—to share with someone, to exercise fellowship) is used instead of the word *give* (Galatians 6:6). What significant truth do you think is conveyed by the specific use of this word?

_____

_____

_____

_____

_____

_____

It's time to order your next study. Allow enough time to get the books so you can distribute them at the Open House. Consider ordering 2-3 extra books for newcomers.

ADDITIONAL INSIGHTS

10. a. The phrase **Do not be deceived** (Galatians 6:7) introduces a solemn warning against living in the flesh. Do you think Christians are exempt from this warning because they are forgiven of all their sins, or are they subject to this spiritual principle in the same way as the unsaved? Explain your answer.

_____

_____

_____

_____

_____

_____

b. Are there any areas in your life where you are "sowing to the flesh" but haven't yet reaped God's corresponding chastisement or retribution?

_____

If so, what can you expect based upon the promised warning in Galatians 6:7?

_____

_____

_____

ADDITIONAL INSIGHTS

ELEVEN

GRACE AND THE CROSS

The final lesson in this study focuses on the consequences of living by faith or in the flesh. Paul warns the Galatian believers that they will reap what they sow (Galatians 6:7–8). The apostle offers one last warning to help the Galatian believers resist the religious solicitation for legalistic living. He closes this important letter with a simple statement of the price he paid to remain faithful to the true gospel (Galatians 6:17, **I bear in my body the marks of the Lord Jesus**). May all who claim the name of Christ be willing to stay true to the gospel, even if it means suffering for His sake.

Before you begin, please pray that God would reveal Himself to you through His Word and give you the grace to accept the spiritual truths you will be learning.

Final Exam:

Are you meeting next week to study the Final Exam? To learn how to present it effectively, contact Lamplighters.

———

ADD GROUP INSIGHTS BELOW

1. The phrase **one who sows to his flesh** (Galatians 6:8) is often thought to refer to the riotous living of the unsaved or carnal Christians. While the phrase applies to everyone who continually attempts to satisfy the cravings of the flesh, to whom does the phrase primarily refer?

    _____

    _____

2. In the phrase **he who sows to the Spirit will of the Spirit reap everlasting life** (Galatians 6:8) appears to teach "works

salvation." What do you think this phrase is teaching?

_____

_____

_____

_____

_____

3. a. The believer is deceived when he allows himself to be puffed up with pride (Galatians 6:3). In what way(s) do you think a Christian deceives himself when he sows to the flesh (Galatians 6:7–9)?

    _____

    _____

    _____

    _____

    b. It is possible for believers to be deceived by Satan during a time of active service for God. Name two specific temptations believers face when they are actively serving God (Galatians 6:9; 1 Kings 19:1–18; Romans 11:2–4).

    _____

    _____

    _____

4. What were the two reasons the Judaizers wanted the Galatians to accept circumcision (Galatians 6:12–13)?

    _____

    _____

    _____

    _____

5. The apostle Paul wore the physical scars of his faith in Christ (Galatians 6:17). No doubt he was referring to the scars that he had received as a servant of the Lord (2 Corinthians 11:23–28).

   a. Why do you think he would refer to them as brand-marks?

   _____

   _____

   _____

   b. What evidence is there in your life of your allegiance and devotion to Christ?

   _____

   _____

   _____

6. Explain the purpose of the Mosaic Law and the believer's present relationship to it.

   _____

   _____

   _____

   _____

   _____

7. As you reflect on the characteristics of grace living and legalism, do you believe you have been living under grace or Law?

   _____

   _____

   _____

   _____

Having trouble with your group? A Lamplighters trainer can help you solve the problem.

ADDITIONAL INSIGHTS

8. In one complete sentence explain the message of the book of Galatians.

_____

_____

_____

9. List the main truths that were taught in this study of Galatians.

_____

_____

_____

_____

10. a. Look closely at each of the following words. Circle only the words that represent your true identity in Christ.

brethren	sons	slaves of sin
heirs with Christ	children of bondage	children of promise
free	crucified with Christ	secure
forgiven	child of darkness	child of light
unconditional love from God	saved by good works	redeemed by God's grace

b. Now look at this second set of words closely. (List continues on next page.) Circle only the words that should characterize a believer's walk or life with God.

liberty	live by the flesh	license
walk in the Spirit	adultery	gentleness
covetousness	selfish ambition	love
drunkenness	goodness	faithfulness

lewdness	idolatry	joy
self-control	hatred	dissensions
peace	patience	jealousy
outbursts of anger/wrath	kindness	gentleness

• • • •

Congratulations,

You have just finished a challenging study of the book of Galatians. But even though this inductive Bible study has been completed, you must stand firm in the freedom Christ has given you. To do this, you need to learn how to "walk in the Spirit" (Galatians 5:16). But remember, don't use your freedom for an opportunity for the flesh, but by love serve others for the glory of God.

Would you like to learn how to lead someone through this same study? It's not hard. Go to www.Lamplighters USA.org to register for *free* online leadership training.

ADDITIONAL INSIGHTS

LEADER'S GUIDE

Lesson 1: Don't Mess with the Gospel

1. a. The Christian Emancipation Proclamation.
    b. The country of the Gauls.

2. Paul and Barnabas were sent out by the church in Antioch to preach the gospel. They traveled to Cyprus and Galatia in southern Asia Minor before returning to the church at Antioch. While they were at Antioch, some Jewish teachers came to the church and began teaching the Galatian Gentiles (non-Jews) that they had to accept the Old Testament Law (or covenant) to be saved. When Paul and Barnabas could not convince these Jewish teachers that the Gentiles did not need to accept the Mosaic law to be saved, it was decided that Paul, Barnabas, and others (including Titus, probably as a test case) should go to Jerusalem and meet with the apostles to discuss the matter. The apostles agreed with Paul and his position, but the false teachers continued to teach their heresy throughout the churches. Paul's letter to the Galatians was written to provide a historical account of the meeting with the apostles in Jerusalem and re-instruct the believers on the necessity of living by grace.

3. a. Yes.
    b. Church membership, baptism (infant or adult, sprinkling, or immersion), denominational affiliation, religious experience, a generic belief in God without trusting in Jesus Christ alone for eternal life, good deeds, keeping the Ten Commandments, sacraments, tithing, confirmation, confession of sins, circumcision. Other answers could apply.

4. a. God must extend grace to an individual, and the individual must receive His grace before genuine peace can be experienced. Other answers could apply.
    b. Grace is a gift from God that enables an individual to fulfill God's will for his life. God is the only source of grace. Besides being an ancient greeting, the word *peace* is used in Scripture to signify the absence of God's wrath on those who have accepted God's gift of righteousness in the person of Jesus Christ (Romans 5:1). Peace can also refer to

the divine assistance and blessing that believers experience when they live in harmony with God's will for their lives. Since the Galatian believers had already received the positional peace of salvation (i.e., the removal of God's wrath), the peace that Paul refers to in verse 3 is God's continuing endorsement and blessing on those who live according to His will.

5. Christ gave Himself for us that he might redeem us from this present evil age. Christ's deliverance is twofold—believers are delivered from the penalty of sin (eternal punishment and judgment) and the power of sin through the indwelling of the Holy Spirit (Romans 7:25–8:17)

6. Everyone who is saved is saved by the grace of God.

7. a. False religious leaders had infiltrated the Galatian churches and taught a continuing obligation to the Old Testament Mosaic Law. The Galatian Christians had accepted their teaching and were trying to fulfill the Law as a means of spiritual growth. While their motives were right and they thought they were being faithful to Christ, they were actually deceived and in the process of deserting Christ—the very One who had rescued them from the curse of the Law.

   b. 1. They were religious teachers who upset the faith of new Christians by teaching that circumcision was necessary for all believers (Galatians 1:7; 4:17; 6:12–13).

      2. They were hypocrites because they expected others to keep the law even though they did not keep it themselves (Galatians 6:12–13).

      3. They were compromisers because they wanted the believers to keep the Law so that they would not be persecuted (Galatians 6:12).

      4. They were proud because they boasted in their converts (Galatians 6:13).

      5. They were deceitful because they taught in such a manner that their listeners turned to them rather than to Christ (Galatians 4:17).

8. a. 1. False teaching disturbed or upset the faith of some (Galatians 1:7).

      2. False teaching produces wild theological speculations that cannot be proved and do not help those who hear them.

3. False teaching causes people to turn away from the truth because they become discouraged and confused over what it right.

4. False teaching leads people to accept myths (unsubstantiated religious beliefs). The listeners have no solid basis upon which to determine what is right because false teachers often deceive by saying that they have received special revelation from God.

b. God the Father.

9. a. Jesus Christ came to deliver man from eternal death and this present evil world (Galatians 1:4). The false religious teachers perverted or distorted the gospel of Jesus Christ that gives man the freedom to escape the bondage of a religious system that does not give peace and the assurance of sins forgiven. Rather than leading their followers to freedom in Christ, they lead them in the opposite direction into bondage, fear, guilt, and enslavement.

b. Paul said that if a person (any person) preached a gospel message other than salvation by grace alone, he should be accursed. The word *accursed* (Gk. *anathema*) means dedicated to destruction. Paul said the gospel must be absolutely unaltered. No one, not even an angel from heaven, has the right to change the message of salvation by grace alone. This is a frightening thought when you think of all the other things religious teachers teach about the way to get to heaven.

10. 1. Some Christians appear to receive a measure of spiritual security by placing themselves under a set of religious rules and regulations.

2. Some believers seem to find it easier to continue their pattern of religious ritualism that they established before they were saved.

3. Some believers find it difficult to believe that God will continue to direct and empower their lives through the indwelling ministry of the Holy Spirit.

4. Some believers appear to lack the knowledge of how to live by God's grace.

5. Some believers still feel they must "earn God's favor" and be "doing Christianity," rather than letting Christ live through them. When they do this, it gives them a measure of spiritual accomplishment that salves their weak consciences. Other answers could apply.

11. a. He would not be a servant of God.

b. Fear of witnessing for Christ, hypocritical actions, worldliness, a lack of peace and joy from God, legalism. Other answers could apply.

c. Answers will vary.

Lesson 2: One Message for All Peoples

1. Paul wanted the Galatians to understand that the commission he received to preach the gospel came directly from God and not through human agency. The false teachers who plagued the early church used their identification with the church in Jerusalem (Acts 15:24) and human endorsement (letters of commendation; 2 Corinthians 3:1) as their credentials. Paul said his commission came from a higher authority— Almighty God.

2. a. God the Father.
   b. Answers will vary.

3. a. Answers will vary.
   b. Guilt, fear, intimidation, visions or special revelations, Scripture cited out of context, isolation of their followers. Other answers could apply.

4. a. Paul had excelled in Judaism, and the report of his former religious life (vs.13–14) should have helped the Galatians realize that he was not a disgruntled reject who was trying to undermine his former manner of religious worship.
   b. It is likely Paul wanted to demonstrate that the gospel message he preached was given to him by divine revelation. The Judaizers used their association with the apostles in Jerusalem to convince young believers that their perverted gospel was the truth. However, the inclusion of Paul's visit to Jerusalem is evidence that he did not deny the authority of the apostles (Galatians 2:1).

5. a. God revealed Jesus Christ to Paul so that he would preach the gospel to the Gentiles.
   b. God has revealed Jesus Christ to all believers for a similar reason. Christians are to preach the good news of Christ's salvation to all people (Mark 16:15). Christians are to be ambassadors (2 Corinthians

5:20). In addition to being ambassadors for Christ, Christians are to be witnesses for Christ by doing all things for the glory of God (1 Corinthians 6:19–20). Other answers could apply.

6. a. Answers will vary.
   b. Throughout the Christian's life he will face situations in which his thoughts and reasonings conflict with the Word of God. When this happens, the Scriptures instruct believers to rely on the Word of God instead of leaning on their own understanding (Proverbs 3:5). As Christians trust the Word of God instead of their own frail reasonings, God honors His Word and vindicates their faith. As a result, the believers' confidence in the Word of God increases, and they are more willing to trust God the next time there is a discrepancy between their thoughts and the revealed Word of God.

7. The teaching of the Judaizers caused the Christians in Galatia to be disturbed in their faith (v. 7) but the ministry of Paul caused believers to glorify God (v. 24).

8. a. Some teachers had come down from Jerusalem and said that the Gentiles could not be saved unless they accepted the Law (v. 1; submitting to circumcision was evidence that a person accepted the OT Law). Paul and Barnabas disagreed with these teachers, and when the conflict could not be resolved in the church at Antioch, Paul and others went to Jerusalem to discuss the matter with the apostles.
   b. They strongly disagreed with them.

9. Answers will vary.

Lesson 3: Avoid Legalism

1. He was fearful that he might have been running or had run in vain (v. 2). Although the phrase appears to indicate that Paul might have been having some second thoughts or doubts about the gospel he was preaching, this interpretation seems unlikely. In the first chapter Paul was dogmatic that the gospel he had been given was a revelation from Jesus Christ (Galatians 1:11–12). If the visit to Jerusalem in Galatians 2 is the same visit made by

Paul, Barnabas, and others in Acts 15 (see Introduction), then Paul was describing in detail the conversion of the Gentiles only a few days prior to his arrival in Jerusalem (Acts 15:3). It seems more likely that he was fearful that his missionary work could be severely damaged if the apostles disagreed with his understanding of the sufficiency of grace. Perhaps he wondered if the Judaizers did receive their "gospel" from the apostles or if the strong Jewish atmosphere in the Jerusalem church had influenced the thinking of its leaders.

2. a. Titus, a Greek (v. 3), was under no obligation to be circumcised prior to his salvation. Now as a Christian leader, if he submitted to circumcision, it might lead others to believe that Christians were obligated to keep the OT Law. This would hinder the true gospel message of salvation by grace apart from the Law.

   b. Paul is saying that the true character of the gospel (the nature and freedom from the Law) would become confused in their thinking if Titus submitted to circumcision. If Titus had become circumcised and news of this got back to Galatia, the brethren might have understood this action as teaching the necessity of the Law for salvation or sanctification.

3. The leaders or pillars (v. 9) of the Jerusalem church did not change or add to the gospel Paul was preaching.

4. a. 1. God has given individual believers different ministry responsibilities within the church. Christians should be careful to realize that God has given His children different backgrounds, abilities and spiritual gifts to be used in a special way for His service (1 Corinthians 12:19–25).

      2. Although individual believers have been given different ministries, the same message of salvation through grace must be preached (v. 7), and certain responsibilities are required (v. 10).

      3. Even though we have been given different individual ministries, God's grace is sufficient for every personal ministry (v. 8).

      4. A correct understanding of the diversity of God's working through Christians should lead to cooperation instead of competition among God's people (v. 9).

   b. The poor. Personal responses will vary.

5. a. When Peter came to the church at Antioch, he ate with the Gentiles. This indicated that Peter believed there was no difference between the Jews and the Gentiles. It also indicated he believed that believers were no longer responsible to the OT Law. However, when some Jews came to the church in Antioch, Peter stopped eating with the Gentiles because he was afraid of the possible reaction from the Jews. Peter's hypocrisy would have raised a question in the minds of the Gentile believers about the need for continuing obligation to the Law.
   b. Peter was afraid of the reaction from the Jews (v. 12).
   c. Division (v. 13), hypocrisy (v. 13), damaged personal testimonies for Peter and Barnabas.

6. Peter's actions were done in public causing other believers to join him in hypocrisy (vs. 12–13). Because of the public nature of Peter's sin and the division caused within the church at Antioch, Paul had to confront the situation publicly in order to expose Peter's error and restore unity to the church. The first Scripture reference (Matthew 18:15) explains the first step believers should take when they learn of continuing private sin in the life of a believer. The second reference (Galatians 6:1) explains the attitude believers should have when they confront another believer who persists in sinful conduct.

7. Man is not justified by the works of the Law and by the works of the Law shall no flesh be justified.

8. a. No.
   b. Christ died needlessly.

9. Victory in the Christian life is not accomplished by the adoption and determined execution of a list of religious responsibilities. When a person comes to Christ, he dies to his old self and becomes alive in Christ. Instead of trying to live for God, the believer should simply allow Christ to live through him. It is the exchange principle—the believer gives up all attempts at self-righteousness and receives God's righteousness in exchange for Christ's complete Lordship in his life. The results are joy, as the believer ceases his striving; peace, as the believer finally finds rest in Christ (Hebrews 4:1–9); and fruitfulness, as the believer stops trying to manufacture ministry and yields to Christ's will in every aspect of life.

10. While the Bible teaches believers are to live for God, the means of doing this is to walk in the Spirit, which is essentially synonymous with letting Christ live through them (Galatians 2:20).

Lesson 4: Sons of Abraham

1. You foolish Galatians (v. 1), who has bewitched you (v. 1), are you so foolish? (v. 3). Paul's use of the word *Galatians* is significant because he does not address a group of believers with such general terminology anywhere else in the New Testament.

2. a. The Galatians believed that Christians reached spiritual maturity by submitting to the OT Law. They had taken their eyes off the Lord Jesus Christ.

   b. Before a Christian can be negatively affected by false teaching, he must fail to analyze or to think through the spiritual ideas and concepts being presented to him. When the word 'foolish' is used to describe a person, it means that he is demonstrating a lack of mental concentration or discernment. If a person fails to discipline his mind to critique the ideas that others present to him, he will inevitably fall prey to dangerous philosophies. As a result of his folly, he could experience personal harm.

3. a. Paul's original ministry to the Galatians clearly presented the person and crucifixion of Christ. Paul's ministry to the churches was always open and above reproach (2 Corinthians 3:1–2; 1 Thessalonians 2:3–12; etc.) in contrast to the ministry of the Judaizers, which was characterized by subversion and deceit (Philippians 3:2–3; 2 Corinthians 11:13–15). Paul publicly presented the "whole counsel of God" by preaching the crucifixion of Christ. Often, Christians can become preoccupied with the ethical teaching of Christ and forget the real reason for Christ's incarnation: to die on the cross for man's redemption (Luke 19:10).

   b. Individuals are saved by hearing the message of salvation and responding in faith.

   c. If man is saved by grace (begun in the Spirit), does he grow in Christlikeness by man-made methods (the flesh, man-made efforts to gain acceptance before God)? In the case of the Galatians it was adherence to the Law. Other answers could apply.

    d. God's continuing work in the life of the believer is a result of faith in God and not adherence to the Law.

4. The Christian must realize that he died to his old self when he accepted Christ. The life he continues to live in the flesh should be an expression of Christ's will on earth. To fulfill Christ's will, he must not try to live for God but allow Christ to live through him (Galatians 2:20). He can only accomplish Christ's will by faith: faith in God's Word, faith in God's presence, faith in God's power, and faith in God's provision. This does not mean he does not incorporate practical steps for spiritual growth. He should begin to study God's Word and pray so that he will understand who God is and how he can please Him. He should become an active part of a local Bible-believing church where he can serve others and fulfill God's plan for his life. Other answers could apply.

5. Persecution (suffering, v. 4). The Greek word for suffering (*pascho*) can mean "to experience evil or suffering" or it can be used in a neutral sense "to experience". However, it is probably best to understand the word to mean "suffer" for two reasons:

    1. Paul and others had suffered persecution in the same region (Acts 13–14).

    2. The actions of the Judaizers were partially motivated by fear of persecution (Galatians 6:12). These two facts support the idea that at least some of the motivation for deserting God came from persecution.

6. The believer.

7. a. The curse of the Law.

    b. Answers will vary.

8. 1. Christ's death on the cross provided redemption for man by releasing him from the curse of the Law.

    2. Man can know that he has been redeemed by Christ (v. 13, **redeemed**; Greek verb tense shows completed or finished action).

    3. Faith in Christ allows Christians to experience some of the blessings of the Abrahamic covenant (v. 14).

    4. All those who have trusted Christ by faith receive the Holy Spirit (v. 14).

Lesson 5: The Purpose of the Law

1. a. Through Jesus Christ.
    b. The giving of the OT (Mosaic) Law.

2. God is able to fulfill His promises even if the completion of such takes thousands of years. God's continuing faithfulness to the Abrahamic covenant teaches that God can be trusted to fulfill His promises of blessing and judgment. Nothing can prevent the fulfillment of God's promises. Other answers could apply.

3. a. 1. Even though the Mosaic Law was given to man many years ago, it has not always been in existence (it was added). The Law was not originally given to man in the beginning so it should not be looked upon as having always been a part of man's existence.
        2. One of the main purposes of the Law ceased when Christ came (**till the seed** [Christ] **should come**, v. 19). Paul is saying that the Law had a beginning and an end. However, this does not mean that the Law does not serve any purpose (1 Timothy 1:8–10; 2 Timothy 3:16–17).
    b. The first coming of Jesus Christ. Specifically, the Law continued to be in force as a national legal code until Christ's death on the cross. Christ ministered under the jurisdiction of the Law (Matthew 8:4; Galatians 4:4) and fulfilled the Law (Romans 10:4, the word end is *telos* which means end, fulfillment or completion). When Christ died on the cross the veil in the temple was rent in two (Matthew 27:51), giving man access to God through the offering of Christ's sacrifice (Hebrews 10:19-21).

4. a. The Law.
    b. God the Father.
    c. None.
    d. No.

5. No.

6. As a tutor or instructor to help man understand the standard of righteousness God demands (vs. 22–24). Secondly, the Law serves to show man that he needs a sin substitute. Thirdly, the Law serves as an ethical standard for

the general harmony of society and individuals in particular. Lastly, the Law serves to show the consistency of the character of God because His standard for ethical behavior is similar in both the Old and New Testaments.

7. a. Son or child of God.
    b. 1. He is baptized or immersed into Christ (v. 27). 2. He is clothed with Christ (a reference to being clothed with the righteousness of Christ, v. 27; 2 Chronicles 6:41; Psalm 132:9). 3. He becomes one of the offspring of Abraham (v. 29). 4. He becomes a part of a new corporate group (v. 28).

8. The subject of Galatians 3 is man's relationship to God. There is nothing in this chapter dealing with administration of the church. Galatians 3:28 teaches God accepts all who come to Him through faith in Christ. God is not concerned if the person is a Jew or a Gentile, a slave or free man or male or female. As the old saying goes, "The ground is level at the foot of the cross." Galatians 3:28 was a rebuke to those in the Galatian churches who were teaching that God would only accept someone if they became a Jew. Using this verse as support for the inclusion of women in the role of pastoral leadership is a failure to follow sound hermeneutical principles (the laws of interpretation). The inclusion or noninclusion of women in positions of pastoral responsibility should be determined by the texts that deal specifically with local church administration (1 and 2 Timothy and Titus). In 1 Timothy, the apostle Paul tells Timothy the purpose for his letter is to instruct Timothy how to administer the church according to God's plan (1 Timothy 3:15). In 1 Timothy 2:8–3:16, he gives specific instruction regarding the roles of men and women in the church. When the roles of men and women in the church are given (1 Timothy 2:9–12), Paul supports his instruction that women are to refrain from teaching men (v. 12) with the argument that reaches far beyond the culture of the day (vs. 13–15). Paul uses the creative order of man (v. 13) and the transgression of Eve to instruct the church about the role of women in the congregational gatherings. Because a woman is not to teach or usurp authority over a man, a woman should not serve in the role of pastoral leadership over men.

Lesson 6: Sons or Slaves?

1. a. Similarities:
    1. Both the child and slave were under constant supervision.
    2. Neither the child nor the slave were not able to experience all the benefits afforded others in the family.
    3. Both the child and the slave were at the mercy of the father's commands.

    Dissimilarities:
    1. The slave has no hope, but the unadopted child has some hope.
    2. The child might inherit everything, but the slave will inherit nothing.

    b. It is a reference to the spiritual condition of the Jews under the age of the Law (v. 5) or the spiritual condition of all men prior to salvation. The use of the pronoun *we* (vs. 3, 5) makes either interpretation possible.

2. 1. Jesus Christ came at the exact time in history appointed by God the Father.
   2. Jesus Christ had a heavenly origin; a proof of His deity.
   3. Jesus Christ was born of a woman; a proof of His humanity.
   4. Jesus Christ was born and ministered under the jurisdiction of the Mosaic Law.

3. God sent His Son at the exact time in history appointed by the Father. Just as the Roman father appointed the time for his son, the heavenly Father appointed the time for Jesus Christ to come to earth. Roman domination of the ancient world allowed free travel and relative safety that aided the early missionaries on their travels. Greek culture and language allowed the early church to spread the gospel with relative ease. Many old religions had died out and many strange new Greek mystery cults had left many people spiritually bankrupt and open to truth. Historians tell us that the ancient Roman world was in great expectation of some sort of deliverance.

4. a. Christ was born, lived, and ministered under the Law.
   b. The gospels provide the record of the incarnation of Jesus Christ. While the presentation of His life is the dominant factor in the gospels, it is important to remember that Jesus ministered under the Law. The gospels are a bridge between the Old and New Testaments and have a very strong connection to the Mosaic Covenant. Often Jesus told an

individual to go and show himself to the priest when he was healed. Under the new covenant, believers are not required to go through a priest because Jesus Christ Himself serves a high priest (Hebrews 9:11, 25). Jesus' statement that He did not come to abolish the Law but to fulfill it is often misunderstood as a mandate to the church for continuing adherence to the Mosaic Law (Matthew 5:17–19). However, what Christ was saying was that He came to minister under the Law as a fulfillment rather than be a rebel. Christ has redeemed us from the curse of the law (Galatians 4:5) and all believers are to live under grace (Romans 6:14).

5. a. The precious blood of Jesus Christ.
    b. 1. The adoption as sons (v. 5). 2. The permanent possession of the Holy Spirit (v. 6). 3. A future inheritance (v. 7; an heir).

6. a. 1. Sons of disobedience (v. 2). 2. Children of wrath (v. 3).
    b. 1. He is separated from Christ. 2. He is excluded or alienated from the commonwealth of Israel. 3. He is a stranger to the covenants of promise. 4. He has no hope (i.e., in relationship to eternal acceptance and blessing). 5. He is without God in this world (he does not experience the direct blessing of having a personal relationship with God during his earthly life).
    c. Answers will vary but should include the following: meaningful personal and corporate worship, righteous living, witnessing.

7. When a Christian understands that his relationship with God is one of unconditional love, his relationship with God should be characterized by love for God and a sincere desire to please Him. The believer will then demonstrate a personal spiritual initiative to do the things that are pleasing to God. This spiritual motivation should not be to gain acceptance before God (this has already been accomplished through Christ). The believer's life should be characterized by spiritual confidence and faith since he knows that God delights in His children and accepts them unconditionally. The believer's general attitude toward his Heavenly Father should be characterized by love rather than by fear and guilt. Other answers could apply.

8. a. Now that God has saved you, why would you want to go back to those

things (fear, bondage, guilt, sin) that you have been saved from? Other answers could apply.

b. The OT Law was weak and beggarly in the sense that it could not save anyone.

c. These words are used to emphasize the point that the OT Law is not able to save anyone. It is weak and beggarly in that sense.

Lesson 7: Promises, Promises

1. He was fearful that all his missionary work among the Galatian churches would be ruined.

2. a. 1. "I urge ..." (an expression of compassionate appeal).
      2. "You have not injured me ..." (this is not a personal offense).
      3. "You received me as an angel from God, even as Jesus Christ."
      4. "My little children" (deep expression of fatherly love).
      5. "I would like to be present with you" (sincere longing to be with them).
      6. "... and to change my tone" (Paul received no personal pleasure by confronting them).
      7. "I have doubts about you" (their spiritual conduct was confusing).
   b. Answers will vary.

3. The sense of blessing which is the joy and confidence that comes from God to the believer who lives by grace. A loss of spiritual joy is an indication that a believer has taken his eyes off Jesus Christ and is not living by grace.

4. a. The false teachers had successfully isolated the Galatian Christians to their own doctrine. The believers were now looking to these teachers rather than to Christ for their spiritual nourishment. The original objective of these false teachers was to create a spiritual bondage in the Galatian Christians, and their goal was accomplished. The Galatian Christians had become totally dependent on these teachers for all spiritual instruction.

   b. Personal prophecies and visions, guilt, fear, intimidation, other authorities, Scripture twisting, worldly promotional methods, etc. Other answers could apply.

5. No. Paul's use of the OT passage in Galatians 4 does not give believers license to assign hidden meanings to other portions of God's Word. Countless erroneous interpretations and heresies have resulted from this dangerous practice. We must remember that Paul, as well as all biblical writers, was writing under the inspiration of the Holy Spirit (2 Peter 1:20–21). If a believer allegorizes or spiritualizes (the assigning of a hidden meaning to the plain reading and intent of the original meaning of Scripture), the meaning and truth of the passage is either missed entirely or distorted significantly. Let's remember Paul's admonition to the Corinthians, "For we write nothing else to you than what you read and understand, and I hope you will understand until the end" (2 Corinthians 1:13 NASB). In other words, don't read between the lines of Scripture or over the top of the lines of Scripture. A helpful saying has guarded many Christians from this serious error, "If the plain sense (of Scripture) makes common sense, seek no other sense."

6. a. Slavery/bondage.
    b. Fear and trembling. Loss of blessing.

7. a. Children of promise. The believer has been adopted by God at the time of salvation and will never return to his or her prior status or condition. Colossians 1:13 says God delivered us (believers) from the power of darkness and transferred us into the kingdom of the Son of His love (Christ). Notice the past tense of the verbs *deliver* and *transfer*, used to indicate the deliverance and transfer took place in the past at the time time of salvation.
    b. Answers will vary.

8. The bondwoman and her son were cast out (v. 30). Paul's use of the OT reference teaches Christians that they cannot become spiritually mature unless they cast out the desire to live for God by trying to keep the Law. Law and grace cannot coexist in the life of a believer without conflict. The believer must deliberately cast out the Law as a means of spiritual sanctification and learn to live by grace alone. God will not fail the believer who makes this bold and essential decision.

Lesson 8: Liberty or License?

1. Liberty is the spiritual state in which the believer is mentally unshackled from all religious attempts to gain acceptance with God and others. The believer is given freedom at the time of salvation and experiences this continuing spiritual privilege by living by grace. When the believer realizes that Christ has set him free, worship and service become a privilege rather than just an obligation.

2. a. 1. Christians should continue to remain steadfast in the freedom Christ has given them. They should remember that God has already accepted them in Christ. 2. They should also resist the attempts of religious legalists to bring them into spiritual bondage. The Judaizers of Paul's day spoke of taking the "yoke of the Law." Perhaps it is this yoke that Paul refers to when he calls it a yoke of slavery (Galatians 5:1).
    b. Answers will vary.
    c. Answers will vary.

3. 1. Christ's continuing ministry through the Holy Spirit will be quenched to the point of ineffectiveness.
    2. If Christians place themselves under the Law, they are obligated to keep the whole Law.

4. a. Paul was addressing the unsaved. Notice the phrase **you who attempt to be justified by law** (v. 4); note that the antecedent of the personal pronoun **you** in v. 4 is **every man** (v. 3). The word *justify* is used almost exclusively in Scripture to refer to the salvation of the lost through Christ's sacrifice. It is important to remember that Paul is writing to a group of churches, and the letter would be read publicly to those present, saved and unsaved. Although those who were unsaved were not actually part of the church in a technical sense, Paul's statement would likely have had a powerful effect on them.
    b. If a person places himself under the Law by receiving the rite of circumcision, he has entered a dangerous spiritual path that will lead him away from Christ (v. 3). This detour will keep the unsaved from salvation (Romans 3:20) and rob the believer of his freedom in Christ and make him a debtor to the whole Law. The person who seeks to

be justified by works has been severed from Christ (v. 4). If a person believes that he can be saved by the Law, then he has been severed from Christ since he is looking at an entirely different and incorrect means of salvation.

5. 1. They begin to listen to a man instead of the truth (v. 7).
   2. They become spiritually insensitive to the One who originally saved them (v. 8).
   3. They fail to recognize that an initial toleration of doctrinal error will eventually lead into total bondage and heresy (v. 9).
   4. They will be led into compromise because they are unwilling to bear the reproach of the cross (v. 11).

6. Christians should never allow their freedom in Christ to become an excuse for sin.

7. a. The believer's actions must be motivated by a love for God rather than a self-centered desire to exercise Christian liberty. Their actions should lead to the spiritual advancement of others rather than causing them to stumble.
   b. He is sinning against other Christians and sinning against Christ (v. 12).

8. a. Answers will vary.
   b. Answers will vary.

9. a. Every believer can fulfill the law by loving his neighbor as himself.
   b. Answers will vary.

10. A critical attitude toward others that often manifests itself in a contentious spirit, unkind speech, and a disagreeable attitude.

Lesson 9: Walk in the Spirit

1. The believer should consider his relationship with God as a continuing fellowship, a close communion, and an abiding partnership. Unfortunately, many believers understand the Christian life to be a series of religious responsibilities that are burdensome. This approach to the Christian life fails to comprehend God's ultimate desire for his people—to love Him and to enjoy His presence forever.

2. 1. Christians are to walk or live in a manner worthy of their calling (God's children, Ephesians 4:1).
    2. Christians are to walk or live distinctively Christian lives and be separated from worldly thoughts, goals, and actions (Ephesians 4:17).
    3. Christians are to walk or live in love that means that all their actions are to be governed by loving concern and respect for others (Ephesians 5:2).
    4. Christians are to walk or live in the light of God's truth (Ephesians 5:8).
    5. Christians are to walk or live in wisdom (Ephesians 5:15).

3. To walk in the Spirit means the believer is in constant communion with God, and his thoughts and actions are governed by God's will for his life rather than his sinful nature. It means that he has dedicated his life to God as a living sacrifice (Romans 12:1), is actively resisting the temptations of the world, and constantly allows his mind to be transformed and renewed by the Word of God (Romans 12:2). He is secure in his relationship with God and is seeking to please Him in all that He does. Christ is his ultimate desire, his constant companion, his primary counselor, and his most passionate longing.

4. a. Adultery, fornication, uncleanness, lewdness, idolatry, sorcery, hatred, contentions, jealousies, outbursts of wrath, selfish ambitions, dissensions, heresies, envy, murders, drunkenness, revelries.
    b. "… and the like."

5. a. Answers will vary but could include: television (shows, commercials, movies), videos, pornography, Internet, music, immoral people, etc.
    b. Answers will vary, but could include not watching television shows, not watching videos or movies that present immoral actions, scenes, or speech. The believer should not look at magazines or books that have nudity, suggestive or immodest pictures or images, immoral or impure articles, stories, etc. The believer should pray for protection for himself and others. Believers who are married should work hard to make and keep their marriages strong. If the believer has a particular area of temptation, he or she should become accountable to a trusted friend. Other answers could apply.

6. a. Covetousness or greed.
    b. Answers will vary.

    c. Confess it as sin and accept God's forgiveness. Don't allow the thing to become an idol in the future.

7. 1. Sorcery (Greek—*pharmakeia*) is the use of drugs for magical or nonmedical purposes or a secret tampering with and worship of the powers of witchcraft. For the believer, this would include a prohibition against a Christian involvement in the occult, astrology, tarot card reading, etc.

    2. Enmity or contentions are hostile feelings, and hatred that is particularly between classes of people, nations, and individuals. This would certainly include all forms of racial prejudice.

    3. Jealousy is the ungodly feeling that an individual experiences when he is envious of what another person possesses. It is an indication of a temporal value system and an unwillingness to trust God.

    4. Dissensions are unresolved conflicts.

    5. Factions are the result of dissensions that ultimately lead to division between parties or groups. They are fueled by gossip, slander, carnality, and anger.

    6. Envy is the desire to deprive another person of what he or she has.

Answers will vary.

8. The person has never been saved and therefore will not enter the kingdom of God.

9. The word *fruit* suggests that the qualities listed in Galatians 5:22–23 are the by-products of grace living. The believer cannot produce these qualities by himself. In him lies no good thing, and without Christ, he can do nothing. The fruit of the Spirit (not man's sinful nature) are manifested in and through the life of the believer naturally when he quits trying to produce godliness and lets Christ live through him. This is an amazing spiritual truth.

10. The believer must learn how to live or walk in the Spirit.

Lesson 10: Living by Grace

1. Sons of God (3:26), Abraham's seed, heirs (3:29), my little children (4:19) and children of promise (4:28).

2. Mature believers (**you who are spiritual**) who are willing to assume their biblical responsibility to love other members of the body of Christ by attempting to restore the ones who are erring.

3. Believers should have a great deal of compassion for those who sin. They should realize that not everyone who is sinning does so with an attitude of willful rebellion. If Christians fail to understand this important truth, it will be difficult for them to demonstrate the gentleness and compassion needed to restore an erring believer. They will be tempted to see every act of sin as willful rebellion. Even though some believers are caught (v. 1) or enticed (James 1:14; Gk. *deleadzo*—to trap or catch by use of bait) into sinful conduct, God still holds them personally responsible for their sin. God has promised that He will never allow the believer to be tempted beyond his power to resist (1 Corinthians 10:13).

4. a. After careful self-reflection, the Christian should go to the erring believer in a spirit of gentleness with the objective of restoring him to Christ.
   b. Gossip, slander, anger, resentment, judging, bitterness, rejection (physical or emotional), avoidance, silence, covering up or ignoring the sin, bitterness. Other answers could apply.
   c. Answers will vary.

5. A competent medical doctor uses skill and exercises extreme care when he sets a patient's broken bone. He shows compassion to the individual, realizing that the patient is undergoing a degree of pain during the restoration of the bone to its original position. Christians should understand they are helping erring believers be restored to spiritual health. The same skill, tenderness, and compassion should be exhibited in the restoration of God's people to a place of spiritual health.

6. Every believer should be willing to bear the normal load of trials and difficulties that are a part of living in a fallen world (Job 5:7; 14:1; John 16:33). In addition to the normal trials and pressures of life, there will be times when God's people are overburdened and need the help of others. Christians are commanded to reach out and become burden bearers. Christians can bear the burdens of other believers by offering emotional support, biblical counsel, material resources (James 2:15–16), etc.

7. The law of the Spirit of life (Romans 8:2), the royal law (James 2:8), the law of liberty (James 2:12).

8. Humility, love, patience, gentleness, diligence, faithfulness. Other answers could apply.

9. a. God's people should assume the responsibility of sharing material things with those who teach God's Word.

   b. The remuneration that a spiritual leader receives should not be considered a gift. It is part of a mutual fellowship in which both parties (the spiritual teacher and the recipient of the teaching) benefit from reciprocal expressions of sharing. The spiritual leader shares what God has entrusted to him (i.e., spiritual understanding of the Word), and the believer shares what God has entrusted to him (material resources). When spiritual teachers do not study diligently in order to present spiritual truth to God's people, they are failing to participate in this fellowship. In the same way, God's people fail to participate in this fellowship when they do not share their material things.

10. a. Although Christians are eternally forgiven for their sins, they experience the law of sowing and reaping. The law of sowing and reaping has three aspects: (1) You reap what you sow, meaning you will likely reach consequences in the same area that you violated God's Word; (2) You reap later than you sowed—just because someone sins and does not immediately receive consequences, that does not mean God is not watching; and (3). You often receive more than you sow.

    b. Answers will vary.

Lesson 11: Grace and the Cross

1. Christians who forfeit the opportunity to give to the work of the Lord and invest in temporal things that cannot satisfy (v. 6).

2. The Christian who willingly invests in the eternal (i.e., supporting God's work) will also reap a spiritual harvest. The support of pastors, missionaries and other Christian workers enables the Word of God to be spread to a lost world. The result will be the salvation of the lost through the preaching of

the Word and rewards for the laborers (both those who helped support the work of the Lord and those who went to preach).

3. a. He is deceived into thinking that the acquisition of material goods can bring him true satisfaction. When a Christian sows to the flesh, he is deceived because his choices indicate that he does not really believe there will be a day of judgment (1 Corinthians 3:10–15; 2 Corinthians 5:10; Romans 14:12). He is investing in what he cannot keep and forfeiting the opportunity to invest in what he cannot lose. He is trying to gain what will not satisfy and forsaking the only means of true satisfaction.

    b. 1. The temptation to believe not all the Christian's efforts will be rewarded (v. 9).

        2. The temptation to believe they are all alone in the fight against evil (1 Kings 19:1–18).

4. So the Galatians would not be persecuted (v. 12), and so the teachers could glory or boast that the Galatians had been converted to their religious position (v. 13).

5. a. Paul uses this word to signify that his scars were evidence of Christ's ownership. They reminded Paul of the important truth that he was not his own and had been bought with a price—the precious blood of Jesus Christ (1 Corinthians 6:19–20).

    b. Answers will vary.

6. The purpose of the Mosaic Law is to point people to Christ. It shows them the unattainable standard of God's righteousness and motivates them to look for another means of salvation. In this sense, it is a tutor or handmaid who nurtures man prior to the time of salvation. The believer has no continuing responsibility to the Mosaic Law (Romans 6:14; Galatians 4:4–5). This does not mean that the Christian should ignore studying the Law, for all Scripture is profitable (2 Timothy 3:16–17).

7. Answers will vary.

8. Since the Christian has been set free, he should live by the grace, which alone will give him power over the flesh. Other answers could apply.

9. Answers will vary.

10. a. brethren, sons, heirs with Christ, children of promise, free, crucified with Christ, secure, forgiven, child of light, unconditional love from God, redeemed by God's grace
    b. Liberty, walk in the Spirit, gentleness, love, goodness, faithfulness, joy, self-control, peace, patience, kindness, gentleness

ADDITIONAL INSIGHTS

FINAL EXAM

Every person will eventually stand before God in judgment—the final exam. The Bible says, **And it is appointed for men to die once, but after this the judgment** (Hebrews 9:27).

May I ask you a question? *If you died today, do you know for certain you would go to heaven?* I did not ask if you're religious or a church member, nor did I ask if you've had some encounter with God—a meaningful spiritual experience. I didn't even ask if you believe in God or angels or if you're trying to live a good life. The question I *am* asking is this: *If you died today, do you know for certain you would go to heaven?*

When you die, you will stand alone before God in judgment. You'll either be saved for all eternity, or you will be separated from God for all eternity in what the Bible calls the lake of fire (Romans 14:12; Revelation 20:11–15). Tragically, many religious people who believe in God are not going to be accepted by Him when they die.

> **Many will say to Me in that day, "Lord, Lord, have we not prophesied in Your name, cast out demons in Your name, and done many wonders in Your name?" And then I will declare to them, "I never knew you; depart from Me, you who practice lawlessness!"** (Matthew 7:22–23)

God loves you and wants you to go to heaven (John 3:16; 2 Peter 3:9). If you are not sure where you'll spend eternity, you are not prepared to meet God. God wants you to know for certain that you will go to heaven.

> **Behold, now is the accepted time; behold, now is the day of salvation.** (2 Corinthians 6:2)

The words **behold** and **now** are repeated because God wants you to know that you can be saved today. You do not need to hear those terrible words, **Depart from Me ....** Isn't that great news?

Jesus himself said, **You must be born again** (John 3:7). These aren't the words of a pastor, a church, or a particular denomination. They're the words of Jesus Christ himself. You *must* be born again (saved from eternal damnation) before you die; otherwise, it will be too late when you die! You can know for certain today that God will accept you into heaven when you die.

These things I have written to you who believe in the name of the Son of God, that you may* know *that you have eternal life.

(1 John 5:13)

The phrase ***you may know*** means that you can know for certain before you die that you will go to heaven. To be born again, you must understand and accept four essential spiritual truths. These truths are right from the Bible, so you know you can trust them—they are not man-made religious traditions. Now, let's consider these four essential spiritual truths.

Essential Spiritual Truth

#1

The Bible teaches that you are a sinner and separated from God.

No one is righteous in God's eyes. To be righteous means to be totally without sin, not even a single act.

There is none righteous, no, not one;
There is none who understands;
There is none who seeks after God.
They have all turned aside;
They have together become unprofitable;
There is none who does good, no, not one.
(Romans 3:10–12)

...for all have sinned and fall short of the glory of God.
(Romans 3:23)

Look at the words God uses to show that all men are sinners—**none, not one, all turned aside, not one**. God is making a point: all of us are sinners. No one is good (perfectly without sin) in His sight. The reason is sin.

Have you ever lied, lusted, hated someone, stolen anything, or taken God's name in vain, even once? These are all sins.

Are you willing to admit to God that you are a sinner? If so, then tell Him right now you have sinned. You can say the words in your heart or aloud—it doesn't matter which—but be honest with God. Now check the box if you have just admitted you are a sinner.

☐ God, I admit I am a sinner in Your eyes.

Spiritual Death

Eternal Life

Now, let's look at the second essential spiritual truth.

Essential Spiritual Truth

#2

The Bible teaches that you cannot save yourself or earn your way to heaven.

Man's sin is a very serious problem in the eyes of God. Your sin separates you from God, both now and for all eternity—unless you are born again.

For the wages of sin is death.
(Romans 6:23)

And you He made alive, who were dead in trespasses and sins.
(Ephesians 2:1)

Wages are a payment a person earns by what he or she has done. Your sin has earned you the wages of death, which means separation from God. If you die never having been born again, you will be separated from God after death.

You cannot save yourself or purchase your entrance into heaven. The Bible says that man is **not redeemed with corruptible things, like silver or gold** (1 Peter 1:18). If you owned all the money in the world, you still could not buy your entrance into heaven. Neither can you buy your way into heaven with good works.

> *For by grace you have been saved through faith, and that not of yourselves; it is the gift of God, not of works, lest anyone should boast.* (Ephesians 2:8–9)

The Bible says salvation is **not of yourselves**. It is **not of works, lest anyone should boast**. Salvation from eternal judgment cannot be earned by doing good works; it is a gift of God. There is nothing you can do to purchase your way into heaven because you are already unrighteous in God's eyes.

If you understand you cannot save yourself, then tell God right now that you are a sinner, separated from Him, and you cannot save yourself. Check the box below if you have just done that.

☐ God, I admit that I am separated from You because of my sin. I realize that I cannot save myself.

GOOD WORKS
MORALITY
RELIGION
MONEY

Spiritual Death

Eternal Life

Now, let's look at the third essential spiritual truth.

Essential Spiritual Truth

#3

The Bible teaches that Jesus Christ died on the cross to pay the complete penalty for your sin and to purchase a place in heaven for you.

Jesus Christ, the sinless Son of God, lived a perfect life, died on the cross, and rose from the dead to pay the penalty for your sin and purchase a place in heaven for you. He died on the cross on your behalf, in your place, as your substitute, so you do not have to go to hell. Jesus Christ is the only acceptable substitute for your sin.

For He [God, the Father] made Him [Jesus] who knew [committed] no sin to be sin for us, that we might become the righteousness of God in Him.
(2 Corinthians 5:21)

I [Jesus] am the way, the truth, and the life. No one comes to the Father except through Me.
(John 14:6)

Nor is there salvation in any other, for there is no other name under heaven given among men by which we must be saved.
(Acts 4:12)

Jesus Christ is your only hope and means of salvation. Because you are a sinner, you cannot pay for your sins, but Jesus paid the penalty for your sins by dying on the cross in your place. Friend, there is salvation in no one else—not angels, not some religious leader, not even your religious good works. No religious act such as baptism, confirmation, or joining a church can save you. There is no other way, no other name that can save you. Only Jesus Christ can save you. You must be saved by accepting Jesus Christ's substitutionary sacrifice for your sins, or you will be lost forever.

Do you see clearly that Jesus Christ is the only way to God in heaven? If you understand this truth, tell God that you understand, and check the box below.

❏ God, I understand that Jesus Christ died to pay the penalty for my sin. I understand that His death on the cross was the only acceptable sacrifice for my sin.

Spiritual Death

Eternal Life

Essential Spiritual Truth

#4

By faith, you must trust in Jesus Christ alone for eternal life and call upon Him to be your Savior and Lord.

Many religious people admit they have sinned. They believe Jesus Christ died for the sins of the world, but they are not saved. Why? Thousands of moral, religious people have never completely placed their faith in Jesus Christ *alone* for eternal life. They think they must believe in Jesus Christ as a real person and do good works to earn their way to heaven. They are not trusting Jesus Christ alone. To be saved, you must trust in Jesus Christ *alone* for eternal life. Look what the Bible teaches about trusting Jesus Christ alone for salvation.

Believe on the Lord Jesus Christ, and you will be saved.
(Acts 16:31)

...that if you confess with your mouth the Lord Jesus and believe in your heart that God has raised Him from the dead, you will be saved. For with the heart one believes unto righteousness, and with the mouth confession is made unto salvation.... For there is no distinction between Jew and Greek, for the same Lord over all is rich to all who call upon Him. For "whoever calls on the name of the Lord shall be saved.
(Romans 10:9–10, 12–13)

Do you see what God is saying? To be saved or born again, you must trust Jesus Christ *alone* for eternal life. Jesus Christ paid for your complete salvation. Jesus said, **It is finished!** (John 19:30). Jesus paid for your salvation completely when He shed His blood on the cross for your sin.

If you believe that God resurrected Jesus Christ (proving God's acceptance of Jesus as a worthy sacrifice for man's sin) and you are willing to confess Jesus Christ as your Savior and Lord (master of your life), you will be saved.

Friend, right now God is offering you the greatest gift in the world. God wants to give you the *gift* of eternal life, the *gift* of His complete forgiveness for all your sins, and the *gift* of His unconditional acceptance into heaven when you die. Will you accept His free gift now, right where you are?

Are you unsure how to receive the gift of eternal life? Let me help you. Do you remember that I said you needed to understand and accept four essential spiritual truths? First, you admitted you are a sinner. Second, you admitted you were separated from God because of your sin and you could not save yourself. Third, you realized that Jesus Christ is the only way to heaven—no other name can save you.

Now, you must trust that Jesus Christ died once and for all to save your lost soul. Just take God at His word—He will not lie to you! This is the kind of simple faith you need to be saved. If you would like to be saved right now, right where you are, offer this prayer of simple faith to God. Remember, the words must come from your heart.

> **God, I am a sinner and deserve to go to hell. Thank You, Jesus, for dying on the cross for me and for purchasing a place in heaven for me. I believe You are the Son of God and You are able to save me right now. Please forgive me for my sin and take me to heaven when I die. I invite You into my life as Savior and Lord, and I trust You alone for eternal life. Thank You for giving me the gift of eternal life. Amen.**

If, in the best way you know how, you trusted Jesus Christ alone to save you, then God just saved you. He said in His Holy Word, ***But as many as received Him, to them He gave the right to become the children of God*** (John 1:12). It's that simple. God just gave you the gift of eternal life by faith. You have just been born again, according to the Bible.

You will not come into eternal judgment, and you will not perish in the lake of fire—you are saved forever! Read this verse carefully and let it sink into your heart.

> ***Most assuredly, I say to you, he who hears My word and believes in Him who sent Me has everlasting life, and shall not come into judgment, but has passed from death into life.***
> (John 5:24)

Now, let me ask you a few more questions.

According to God's holy Word (John 5:24), not your feelings, what kind of life did God just give you? _____

What two words did God say at the beginning of the verse to assure you that He is not lying to you? _____   _____

Are you going to come into eternal judgment? ☐ YES   ☐ NO

Have you passed from spiritual death into life? ☐ YES   ☐ NO

Friend, you've just been born again. You just became a child of God.

To help you grow in your new Christian life, we would like to send you some Bible study materials. To receive these helpful materials free of charge, e-mail your request to **info@LamplightersUSA.org**.

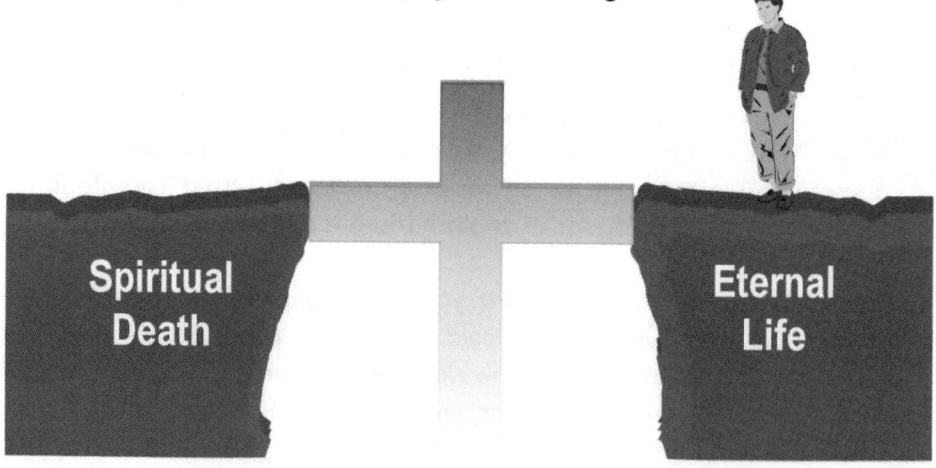

Spiritual Death

Eternal Life

Appendix

Level 1 (Basic Training)
Student Workbook

To begin, familiarize yourself with the Lamplighters' *Leadership Training and Development Process* (see graphic on page 112). Notice there are two circles: a smaller, inner circle and a larger, outer circle. The inner circle shows the sequence of weekly meetings beginning with an Open House, followed by an 8–14 week study, and concluding with a clear presentation of the gospel (Final Exam). The outer circle shows the sequence of the Intentional Discipleship training process (Leading Studies, Training Leaders, Multiplying Groups). As participants are transformed by God's Word, they're invited into a discipleship training process that equips them in every aspect of the intentional disciple-making ministry.

The Level 1 training (Basic Training) is *free*, and the training focuses on two key aspects of the training: 1) how to prepare a life-changing Bible study (ST-A-R-T) and 2) how to lead a life-changing Bible study (10 commandments). The training takes approximately 60 minutes to complete, and you complete it as an individual or collectively as a small group (preferred method) by inserting an extra week between the Final Exam and the Open House.

To begin your training, go to www.LamplightersUSA.org to register yourself or your group. A Lamplighters' Certified Trainer will guide you through the entire Level 1 training process. After you have completed the training, you can review as many times as you like.

When you have completed the Level 1 training, please consider completing the Level 2 (Advanced) training. Level 2 training will equip you to reach more people for Christ by learning how to train new leaders and by showing you how to multiply groups. You can register for additional training at www. LamplightersUSA.org.

Intentional Discipleship
Training & Development Process

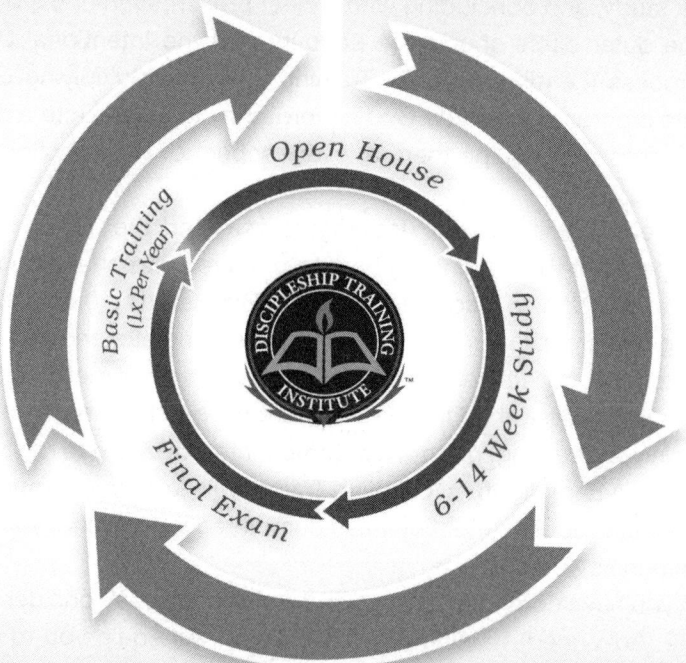

Multiplying Groups

The 5 Steps of Faith for Starting Studies
Training Library
Online Resources

Leading Studies

ST-A-R-T
10 Commandments
Solving All Group Problems

Open House

Basic Training
(1x Per Year)

6-14 Week Study

Final Exam

Training Leaders

4 Responsibilities of a Trainer
Leadership Training

4 Levels of Student Development
3 Diagnostic Questions

John A. Stewart © 2017

How to Prepare a
Life-Changing Bible Study
ST-A-R-T

Step 1: _____ and _____.

Pray specifically for the group members and yourself as you study God's Word. Ask God (_____) to give each group member a rich time of personal Bible study, and thank (_____) God for giving you a desire to invest in the spiritual advancement of each other.

Step 2: _____ the _____.

Answer the questions in the weekly lessons without looking at the

_____ _____.

Step 3: _____and _____.

Review the Leader's Guide, and _____ every truth you missed when you originally did your lesson. Record the answers you missed with a _____ _____ so you'll know what you missed.

Step 4: _____ _____.

Calculate the specific amount of time _____ _____ to spend on each question and write the start time next to each one in the _____ using a _____.

How to Lead a Life-Changing Bible Study

10 COMMANDMENTS

1	2	3
4	5	6
7	8	9
	10	

Lamplighters' 10 Commandments are proven small group leadership principles that have been used successfully to train hundreds of believers to lead life-changing, intentional discipleship Bible studies.

Essential Principles for Leading Intentional Discipleship Bible Studies

1. The 1st Commandment: The _____ Rule.
   The Leader-Trainer should be in the room _____ minutes before the class begins.

2. The 2nd Commandment: The _____-_____ Rule.
   Train the group that it is okay to _____, but they should never be _____.

3. The 3rd Commandment: The _____ Rule.
   _____, _____, _____ ask for _____ to _____ the _____, _____, and _____ the questions. The Leader-Trainer, however, should always _____ the questions to control the _____ of the study.

4. The 4th Commandment: The ____:____ Rule.
   _____ the Bible study on time and _____ the study on time _____ _____. No exceptions!

5. The 5th Commandment: The _____ Rule.
   Train the group participants to _____ on God's Word for answers to life's questions.

1	2	3
4 **59:59**	5	6
7	8	9
	10	

6. The 6th Commandment: The _____ Rule.

Deliberately and progressively _____ _____ participants into the group discussion over a period of time.

7. The 7th Commandment: The _____ _____ Rule.

_____ the participants to get _____ the answers to the questions, not just _____ or _____ ones.

8. The 8th Commandment: The _____ Rule.

_____ the group discussion so you _____ the lesson _____ _____ and give each question _____ _____.

9. The 9th Commandment: The _____-_____ Rule.

Don't let the group members talk about _____ _____, _____ _____, or _____ _____.

10. The 10th Commandment: The _____ Rule.

_____ God to change lives, including _____.

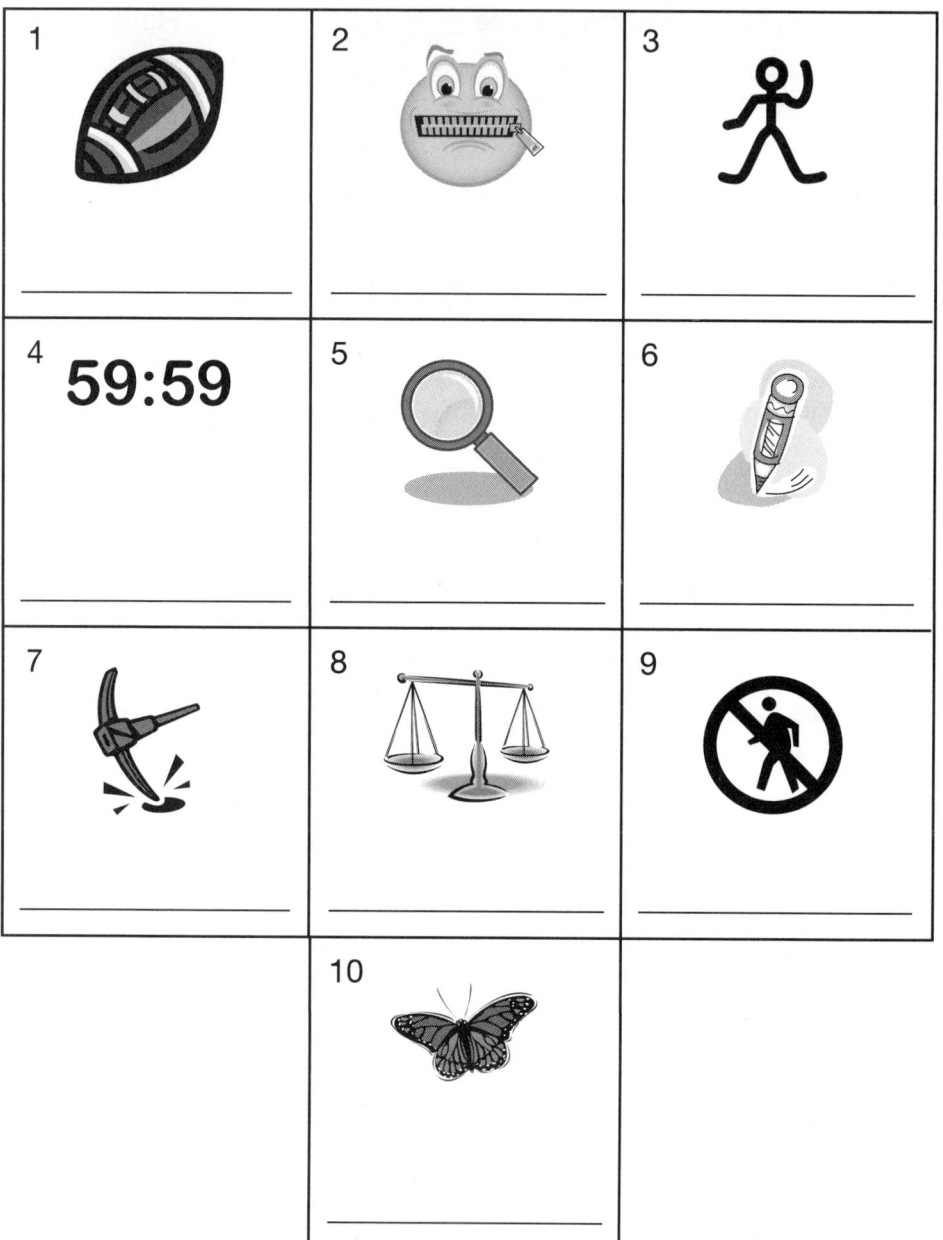

1

2

3

4 **59:59**

5

6

7

8

9

10

Choose your next study from any of the following titles

- John 1-11
- John 12-21
- Acts 1-12
- Acts 13-28
- Romans 1-8
- Romans 9-16
- Galatians
- Ephesians
- Philippians

- Colossians
- 1 & 2 Thessalonians
- 1 Timothy
- 2 Timothy
- Titus/Philemon
- Hebrews
- James
- 1 Peter
- 2 Peter/Jude

Additional Bible studies and sample lessons are available online.

For audio introductions on all Bible studies, visit us online at www.Lamplightersusa.org.

Looking to begin a new group?
The Lamplighters Starter Kit includes:

- 8 James Bible Study Guides
  (students purchase their own books)
- 25 Welcome Booklets
- 25 Table Tents
- 25 Bible Book Locator Bookmarks
- 50 Final Exam Tracts
- 50 Invitation Cards

For a current listing of live and online discipleship training
events, or to register for discipleship training, go to
www.LamplightersUSA.org/training.

Become a Certified
Disciple-Maker or Trainer

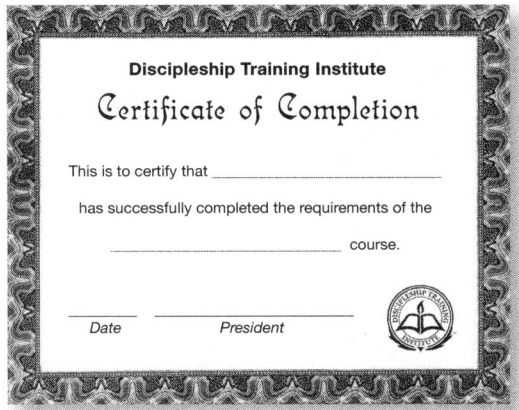

Training Courses Available:

- Leader-Trainer
- Discipleship Coach
- Discipleship Director
- Certified Trainer (Level 1)

Contact the Discipleship Training Institute
for more information (800-507-9516).

The Discipleship Training Institute is a ministry of
Lamplighters International.